BETWEEN GOOD and EVIL

HOW I FINALLY OPPOSED THE KREMLIN PROPAGANDA

MARINA OVSYANNIKOVA

Post Hill PRESS

A POST HILL PRESS BOOK
ISBN: 979-8-88845-050-5
ISBN (eBook): 979-8-88845-051-2

Between Good and Evil:
How I Finally Opposed the Kremlin Propaganda

Cover design by Conroy Accord

All people, locations, events, and situations are portrayed to the best of the author's memory. While all of the events described are true, some names and identifying details have been changed to protect the privacy of the people involved.

Post Hill Press
New York • Nashville
posthillpress.com

Published in the United States of America
1 2 3 4 5 6 7 8 9 10

TABLE OF CONTENTS

CHAPTER 1

PROTEST IS AKIN TO SUICIDE

MARCH 14, 2022

"Three, two, one...Presenter, in the frame!" shouts the director from the studio control room. His voice is tense but firm. An air is like an air, and he had thousands of them. Before my eyes is a wall of monitors.

The program Vremya is on the air. Ekaterina Andreeva is in the studio.

The presenter today is wearing a black jacket and a white T-shirt with a red heart underneath. Every day since the beginning of the war she has worn such T-shirts on the air. Every new day, a new T-shirt and a new heart.

Lines run briskly across the teleprompter screen. Andreeva minted every word:

> *Main events of the day: a strike on civilians. Dozens of people, including children, died in Donetsk after being shelled by Ukrainian nationalists....*

They unlocked Mariupol and began the mass evacuation of civilians, who were actually being held hostage by the neo-Nazis.

Medals of Valor were awarded to eleven other servicemen who distinguished themselves during a special military operation....

The clock struck 9:01 p.m. About an hour more, and that would be the end of the day. In the huge newsroom behind the anchorwoman are several editors. As the camera picks up, you can see them staring intently at their computer screens. Viewers think the people in the studio are watching the airwaves or monitoring the news. In reality, they are shopping online, booking hotels, and looking for a quicker way to avoid evening traffic jams. No outside noises reach Ekaterina Andreeva. Her seat is shielded by a tall glass partition.

Seven meters from the presenter, a policeman sits lazily, tapping on his phone. Outside the newsroom there are two more security posts. Three security guards from Channel One's own security service, dressed in black suits, boredly look around. They know every employee of the Newscasting Directorate by sight, but still ask for a pass every time. There is a barbed wire fence around the TV center and two more rings of security.

Sitting in the small office of an international newsroom, I try to concentrate as I listen to the online broadcast of the UN Security Council meeting on the situation in Ukraine. There are several monitors in front of me with pictures from Reuters, Sky News, and Eurovision. It's war. There are horrific images of destroyed Ukrainian cities, bodies lying motionless on the ground, explosions, and an endless stream of refugees. Channel One has a subscription to these videos and can use them freely, but we only show images sent from the Russian Ministry of Defense, FSB, and filmed by our own correspondents. Our main task is to create a parallel reality and make the war look like an operation to liberate peaceful residents of Donbass. A few minutes before the start of the live broadcast, an intercom call goes out.

"Marina, we have to redo Nebenzya's speech. Take another fragment, about the death of an American journalist," the chief editor of the Vremya program shouts loudly into the receiver.

Vasily Nebenzya is Russia's permanent representative to the UN. He just said that journalist Brent Reno was killed in Irpin by a Ukrainian bullet, not a Russian one. These words urgently need to be aired. Everything that can play against Ukraine is carefully extracted from the vast array of information.

I run to the editing room. A red light flashes on the door of the newsroom. Access to the air broadcast zone is only by special electronic passes. I have one of those.

"We're redoing Nebenzya. I'm going to have to hurry up," I tell the editor while running my eyes over the layout. "The Ukrainian Block is about to end; I don't have much time."

I fly into my office with frantic speed and grabbed my white jacket. In the sleeve of my jacket is a wrapped poster. Inside the newsroom, I take it out and quickly climb up to the podium where the presenter is sitting. Dozens of spotlights hit my eyes.

"On how to mitigate the impact of Western sanctions...," Andreeva reads monotonously.

"*No war! Stop the war!*" I shout, unfurling a huge banner behind her back. I don't recognize my own voice.

Andreeva continues to read nonchalantly from the prompter: "And at a meeting in the government they discussed how to maintain accessibility...."

I understand that another camera is working. The red light is on the left, which means that viewers can't see the poster on the air behind the anchorwoman. I take one step to the left. Now they can see the sign: "No war. Stop the war. Don't believe the propaganda. You are being lied to here. Russians against war."

Out of the corner of my eye I see myself on the monitor, but the picture immediately changes. It was the director in the control room who finally reacted and started some kind of reportage to hide what was going on in the studio. My protest lasted only six seconds.

I walk out of the studio on cotton legs. The blond policewoman flutters her eyelashes in surprise and silently looks in my direction. I walk through the newsroom and drop the poster next to the photocopier that stands under the stairs. The entire management of Channel One's newscasts department is already walking toward me down the corridor.

"Was that you?" is the first question. The deputy head's face is tense, his eyebrows drawn together.

"Yes, it was me," I say. There's no point in denying it.

The head of the Directorate of Information Programs, Kirill Kleimenov, hearing my answer, suddenly turns around and leaves without saying a word.

"Let's go to my office," says Alexei*, his other deputy.

This good-natured-looking man worked for years as NTV's own correspondent in London. We go into his spacious office.

"Would you like some water?" Alexei asks.

I take the glass handed to me. My hands are shaking, and I hardly take a sip. The door opens, a policeman enters the office almost silently, and like a shadow, without saying a word, freezes by the door.

"Do you realize that you set up your colleagues?" Alexei begins.

"It's my personal choice; they have nothing to do with it."

"Do you have some kind of conflict with your colleagues?" he continues.

---

* Name changed

"No, I'm a completely peaceful and conflict-free person."

"Maybe you have relatives in Ukraine?"

"Yes, I have two cousins living in Ukraine. Thank God they are in a safe place. Don't look for personal motives. I have virtually no contact with them and haven't been to Ukraine in twenty years. I was simply protesting against the war, as I consider this war to be the worst crime of the twenty-first century."

"I would have liked to meet you under different circumstances.... But there is no other way out. Write a letter of resignation at your own request," sums up the deputy head.

I refuse to do it without lawyers. Then Alexei asks me to at least write an explanatory letter. I write a few lines:

"I, Marina Vladimirovna Ovsyannikova, do not agree with the information policy of Channel One. I consider the war unleashed by Russia to be the most despicable and horrible crime. And all of you will sit in the dock at the International Criminal Tribunal in The Hague!"

I hand the chief the piece of paper, surprised at my own courage. A few days ago a new article on fakes appeared in the Criminal Code. For an anti-war protest on live television I could be sent to prison for fifteen years.

A policeman leads me out of the office. Behind the doors are several other policemen and security guards from Channel One's internal security service. They look at me with eyes full of horror.

"I need to get my things," I say to the men in uniform.

I am led down a wide corridor with glass partitions. We go into the general editing area. There are ten people inside. There is an expression of fear and confusion on the faces of my colleagues. I notice two employees from the elite department of Garant TV. It is a division that exclusively serves President Vladimir Putin and the top Kremlin officials. Only the most experienced and most vetted people work there. There are similar departments on all the federal channels. Garant TV is an unofficial name, a reference to the Basic Law of the country, which states that the president is the main guarantor of the Constitution. For the sake of keeping Putin in power, the Russian Constitution has already been changed twice.

My colleagues seem to be beginning to realize that they're not going home anytime soon. The investigators will be questioning them all night. There will be no more live broadcasts. All news releases from this day will go with a slight delay.

I take my things and head for the exit.

On the whiteboard is a reminder in large letters from the leadership: "This is not 'WAR,' but a 'SPECIAL MILITARY OPERATION.'"

CHAPTER 2

WHO DO YOU WORK FOR?

Two policemen lead me down the long corridor of the television center.

Meanwhile, the picture of the anti-war protest is already being broadcast by all the leading TV companies in the world. Hundreds of people are writing words of gratitude on social networks. Near Ostankino, as I will be told later, a man is standing with a bouquet of white roses, which he wanted to give me as a sign of gratitude.

We go into the police department, which is located right in the TV center building. There's a lot of commotion inside. The service phones are ringing non-stop. Some plainclothes police arrive. They don't pay the slightest attention to me. I understand that I have not a minute to lose. Unobtrusively, I take my phone out of my bag, open the social networks, and post a video message that I recorded at home:

> What is happening now in Ukraine is a crime. Russia is the aggressor country. And responsibility for this crime lies on the conscience of only one person. And that person is Vladimir Putin.

> My father is Ukrainian, my mother is Russian, and they have never been enemies. The necklace hangs around my neck (in the colors of the Russian and Ukrainian flags) as a symbol that Russia must immediately stop the fratricidal war so that our brotherly peoples can still be reconciled.
>
> Unfortunately, I have been working at Channel One for the past few years, doing Kremlin propaganda, and I am very ashamed of it now. I am ashamed that I allowed lies to be told from the TV screen. I'm ashamed that I let the Russian people be zombified.
>
> We stayed silent in 2014, when all this was just beginning. We did not go to rallies when the Kremlin poisoned Navalny. We just silently watched this anti-human regime. And now the whole world has turned its back on us. And ten more generations of our descendants will not wash away the shame of this fratricidal war.
>
> We, Russian people, thinking and intelligent, only in our power to stop this madness. Come out to the rallies; don't be afraid; they can't put us all in jail.

The video loads very slowly and I look around. I notice that one of the guards is staring in my direction. I instinctively cringe.

"Marina, are you okay? Do you have a lawyer?" a message from a former colleague of mine pops up on the screen. After Putin unleashed the war in Donbass, she left the state television channel Rossiya and joined the opposition. I quickly send her the video.

"Marina, where are you?" I see a message from Igor Riskin, former correspondent of Channel One in Washington. He has been living with his family in the United States for a long time now.

"I'm at the police station in Ostankino," I manage to write. And just in case, I also send him the video.

"Quickly turn off your phone," I hear a demanding male voice. I look up and see a short man in front of me with a black folder under his arm.

"Why did you do it? Did you act alone or did someone help you?"

I tell him the whole truth. I was alone; no one knew about my intentions to go live. When the war started, I had a strong emotional shock; I couldn't eat, drink, or sleep. I wanted to go to Manezhnaya Square, but I saw that the Federal Guard was grabbing everyone who was protesting and throwing them into police vans. Then I decided that I could make a more effective protest.

It was my weekend. I bought a piece of absorbent cotton and markers, and I drew this poster on my kitchen table. Right after that, I recorded a video message. At first I wanted to stand back inside the newsroom, but at the last minute I decided to run right behind the host. I was 90 percent sure that I wouldn't be able to do it; either I wouldn't make it into the studio, or my knees would shake at the last moment, or the director would quickly remove me from the frame.

More and more people come into the office. They are from different power structures, but they ask the same questions:

"Why is the inscription in English?"

"In English, the message for the Western public is that the Russians are against the war; they don't want this war. Only one person needs this war—Vladimir Putin, because he wants to keep power in his hands. And for the Russians who are zombified by propaganda, I wrote very simply, 'You are being lied to here!' I just wanted them not to fall for this propaganda, to look for alternative sources of information. Learn to compare and analyze."

I stop talking for a second. The hands of the clock hanging on the wall are approaching midnight. The investigators are diligently writing something in their reports.

"I want to call a lawyer; give me the phone!" I demand.

They suggest that I go somewhere else to meet the lawyer. We go out the rear entrance of the TV center and get in the car.

"Where are we going?" I wondered aloud.

My sullen companions keep silent. I keep my eyes on the road. On the left are high-rise buildings, and on the right stands the Ostankino TV tower, glowing with advertising lights. The car pulls into the territory of the All-Russia Exhibition Center, which is closed to cars, and stops beside a gray two-story building, hidden from prying eyes by a blind fence. A huge sign on the facade reads, "Police Department."

"Wow," I say. "I've walked these alleys so many times, but I didn't even know that there was a police department in the park."

We enter the building. There's not a soul inside, except for the officer on duty.

"Where is the lawyer?" I glance around the small office, which is piled with papers. My question remains unanswered. The investigator closes the door firmly and starts to explain softly that he is from the Center for Counteraction to Extremism.

"Is this an interrogation? Let me at least call my son. He's worried; I usually get home from work at this time."

"It's not an interrogation; it's just a friendly conversation," the investigator says, smiling like an old friend. "You see, I'm not writing anything. I just want to understand why you did it. Who ordered it?"

"My conscience! Are you familiar with this concept? I am an adult and I make all my decisions on my own. Once again, it was my personal choice. The war was the point of no return. It was no longer possible to remain silent. In the last twenty years Putin has destroyed all independent media in Russia. It all started with the demolition of NTV, then came the elimination of TV Dozhd and Ekho Moskvy, and now there are no opposition media left in Russia. All television is in state hands. After Maidan, Ukraine became the main enemy of the Kremlin. For eight years, the state media have been doing everything possible to dehumanize Ukrainians and make Russians hate them. If we said anything about Ukraine and its inhabitants, we used only the words 'nationalists,' 'followers of Bender,' 'supporters of Right Sector,' and fighters from the Azov regiment. The president of the independent country, Volodymyr Zelensky, was called 'clown,' 'comedian,' and 'drug addict' on the air.

"With the help of controlled media, the Kremlin deceives an entire nation using the Goebbels technique of constantly calling black white. It is this false information that allows it to change the consciousness of the masses. Propaganda is poured into the masses in a continuous stream, day and night, through all channels. No wonder millions of Russians have been turned into hordes of cruel executioners."

I speak quickly, almost without pausing. Anger and indignation grow in my soul by the minute.

"I haven't watched television in ten years, and I can tell you that my colleagues don't watch it either. You understand that the Kremlin propaganda is only believed by poorly educated people from the regions, mostly the elderly, who have never been abroad. Seventy-seven percent of Russians do not even have a passport for travel abroad. According to statistics, only five percent of our fellow citizens have been to Europe or the United

States. No wonder that the majority of Russians believe Putin and think that the West is full of enemies. Have you been to Europe yourself?" I ask the investigator.

He shrugs his shoulders in silence and continues to listen to my monologue.

"I wish I had left Channel One eight years ago," I add. "I guess I was saved by the fact that I worked in the international department. I didn't have to write propaganda texts. I watched CNN, Sky News, Reuters, and APTN. I talked on Skype with political scientists, scholars, and our colleagues from the U.S. and Europe. But the cognitive dissonance of everything that was going on increased every year. I looked with envy at my colleagues, who could give up everything and leave. I could not afford it; I had a difficult divorce, two children, an unfinished house, an elderly mother, a car loan, and a lot of other problems. I was weak, and I could not find the strength to leave TV. The schedule was convenient; I worked one week and rested the next week. That was the schedule of news broadcasting on all the central TV channels. It was ideal to raise children, travel, do sports, and meet with friends. But on the first day of the war, I definitely decided I was going nowhere."

The clock struck five o'clock in the morning. There is a pre-dawn silence outside the window.

"You know, I'm tired. Under Article 51, I don't have to testify against myself. I have to go out...."

The investigator accompanies me to the bathroom door.

"Why are you following me?"

"That's the way it's supposed to be. In case you open your veins there..."

This was not some super-intelligent frontline investigator from Lubyanka, but an ordinary policeman not at all adept at international politics. His phone kept ringing, and I could hear fragments of phrases on the other end of the line.

"Ask her why...and how does she feel?.... Who helped her?...." Invisible interlocutors from high offices located on Staraya Square and Lubyanka are constantly present in our conversation. Apparently, they are trying to decide how to hush up this grand scandal.

"So, is this a criminal case or an administrative one? What do you think?"

"Call me a lawyer; let him explain to me all the nuances. I am, unfortunately, not a lawyer by training." I get irritated, but I realize that irritation does not help. I force myself to calm down.

"Who do you work for?" he repeats again.

"There's no need to look for ulterior motives. It was a normal reaction of a normal person to a criminal war. The fact is that on February 24, each of us had a 'Contract with the Devil' quietly placed on our desks. If you stayed to work for this criminal regime, it means you signed it...."

The investigator looks at me fearfully. I suspect that he is recording my interrogation on video. I speak very honestly and openly. Let them know that protest sentiments have penetrated the "holy of holies"—the main mouthpiece of the Kremlin propaganda program, Vremya.

"But still, who ordered this action? Who paid you?" The investigator would not stop.

"Paid? I don't need anything in particular. I live an ordinary middle-class life in Moscow. I have everything a person needs to be happy—a son, a daughter, a house, dog, car, friends...."

"But that bracelet you have on your arm, what kind is it? Gold?"

"The usual costume jewelry. What are you implying? Do you think that everything in this life is done for money? You are sorely mistaken!"

"I'm still sitting here thinking...administrative or criminal? You want to go to jail?"

"I'm a normal person, and of course, I don't want to go to jail. But anyway, when I decided to protest on the air, I was aware of all the risks. I assumed I would spend two or three years in prison."

It is ten o'clock in the morning. I hear voices outside the door. A young guy brings us coffee in paper cups and pancakes. The investigator asks him to keep an eye on me, and he disappears. I take a sip of coffee, while I watch my guard carefully.

"Oh, Zelensky expressed his gratitude to you," he says suddenly, taking his eyes off the phone. But, embarrassed, he quickly shuts up, realizing that he said too much.

"Great, thanks to Zelensky," I say enthusiastically, "he's a hero who didn't run away from the surrounded Kiev. He stayed with his people even though he was asked to evacuate to Lviv. Not like Putin, who started a criminal war in Europe and is hiding in a bunker."

The interrogator returns; apparently, he has received a new batch of instructions. The tone of the interrogation changes.

"Marina Vladimirovna, why don't you love your homeland?" he asks sharply when we are alone again.

"I do love my homeland. But you must understand that the motherland and the people who are in power now are two completely different things. Look what they have done. Millions of Ukrainian refugees are on the border with Poland, Moldova. These are defenseless women and children. In one day Putin deprived them of everything—homes, housing, jobs. I know what it's like; I went through the same thing when I was a child. My family had to flee Grozny when the first Chechen war broke out there. We were left without an apartment, without things, with absolutely nothing. My mother, at forty years of age, had to start her life from scratch. She still can't recover from this trauma. Those were the nineties, long years of misery, poverty, humiliation. I had a miserable childhood. So I understand very well what the future holds for refugees. The scale of the tragedy is colossal, and you don't understand all of this; you're just sitting in your office. Russia will not wash its shame away for a long time, and your children and grandchildren will pay for this criminal war."

"You are wrong. Putin did everything right. If it weren't for us, the Ukrainians would have been the first to attack us. Besides, the U.S. and NATO are at war against us."

The investigator takes a noisy sip of coffee and continues in an unexpectedly ingratiating voice, looking into my eyes: "Do you want to work for us? You won't need anything."

"Are you kidding me? The people who are now in power disgust me deeply. I'd rather starve to death. To start a war in the twenty-first century, you realize that's really insane...."

"After all, it's a criminal case. You will go to jail," the investigator says firmly, as if answering the question that had tormented him.

"Get a lawyer," I say. I can't hide my irritation anymore.

The investigator comes out again. His partner immediately appears. They don't leave me unattended for a minute. I lie down on the back of the couch, close my eyes, and try to distract myself a little. But the blood pulses in my temples and my consciousness draws the bleakest pictures. I understand that my fate is now being decided in the highest offices.

"Macron offered you political asylum and diplomatic protection," the policeman sitting next to me reads the news feed aloud.

"It can't be." I open my eyes, not fully believing the reality of what is happening. The reaction of the international community is like a straw for a drowning man. I grasp at it, hoping to float.

From the corridor, fragments of the investigator's phrases can be heard: "Got it; that's right. Let's do it."

After a few minutes, he returns and says, "We will go to court soon. We'll try you on an administrative offense."

CHAPTER 3

A GUEST FROM THE FUTURE OF RUSSIA

There are several reporters on duty outside the courthouse. I wave at them from the window of the police car, but they don't see me through the tinted car windows. The police officers lead me into the Ostankinskiy court from the back entrance.

"Hold on, you're a real hero!" whispers an unfamiliar man in the corridor.

I smile back at him. We go up to the third floor and enter the courtroom.

I take a sheet of paper and start writing a petition to postpone the hearing, because I don't have a lawyer. At that moment, a short man with an athletic build rushes into the hall.

"I finally found you." He sighs happily.

Anton Gashinsky, a well-known lawyer from Belarus, quickly starts filling out the necessary paperwork. I tell him that I have a seventeen-year-old son, Kirill, and an eleven-year-old daughter, Arisha, and ask for the phone to call them.

"Kirill. How are you?" I ask my son.

"You should have at least warned us, because we're all standing around." My son's voice sounds unhappy.

"I couldn't have warned you. You would have tried to stop me. Remember last week when I wanted to go to the anti-war protest organized by Navalny's headquarters in Pushkin Square? You hid the keys to my car. I just couldn't keep quiet. Please send me a scan of your sister's birth certificate," I ask my son.

The judge enters the room and I disconnect the call. She quickly reads out the charge under the new administrative article. I am accused of calling unauthorized rallies. They are judging me for the video message I posted on my social networks.

"I don't plead guilty. I don't retract any of my words," I say, trying to hide my excitement.

"There are no grounds for the application of this administrative article," says lawyer Gashinsky, "because it was an abstract call to go to rallies. Marina did not mention the exact date and time when she had to go to the rallies. Besides, she has two minor children who depend on her."

The arguments have no effect on the judge. She finds me guilty of an administrative offense and orders me to pay a fine of thirty thousand rubles.

There is a huge crowd of journalists in front of the Ostankinsky court building.

"I don't want to go there. I'm very tired; can we not talk to the press? Maybe we can find another way out," I ask the lawyer.

"We need to talk to the journalists, just a few phrases, and then we'll quickly get in the car," Gashinsky insists.

I try to gather my thoughts. There are questions in Russian and English on all sides.

"Was it your personal decision or did someone help you?"

"Did you expect such a court decision?"

"I will be ready to answer all your questions tomorrow. I am very tired. I spent two days without sleep. The interrogation lasted more than fourteen hours; they did not give me a lawyer, did not provide any legal assistance, and did not allow me to contact my family and friends," I explain as I continue to move through the crowd of journalists to the small car.

Our car can barely crawl. There is evening traffic on the Garden Ring. We drive to the office of Sergei Badamshin, one of Moscow's most famous political lawyers. A huge American flag is flying ahead. The car pulls up on Novinsky Boulevard, not far from the American Embassy building. Next door in an elite business center are some of the most expensive offices in Moscow. We go up to the eighth floor.

Badamshin, a middle-aged man with an ironic smile, greets us.

"Let's have a brainstorming session," he offers immediately. "At any moment they could initiate a criminal case."

"Maybe I shouldn't go home," I say.

"Of course, we'll hide you."

For another hour we discuss the nuances of the case. Badamshin gives me a temporary phone number and a long list with numbers of almost all the largest TV companies in the world that want to interview me.

"I'll start talking to the press tomorrow. I have absolutely nothing to hide. Right now I just need to rest. I'm not thinking straight," I say.

"The most important thing is not to relax," Badamshin admonishes me at the end. "The reaction will come later when everyone has forgotten about you. Right now it's not profitable for them to make a hero out of you."

The bright advertising lights flash outside the window. The lawyer drives me to the southwest of Moscow. I turn on my phone and read the news headlines. Deutsche Welle, "Marina Ovsyannikova is a guest from the future of Russia," The *Guardian* put a screenshot of the Vremya program on its cover, Marina

Ovsyannikova's name came first on Twitter, Alexei Navalny mentioned what Marina Ovsyannikova did in his last statement at the trial, and politician Ilya Yashin wrote "Marina Ovsyannikova is a Hero of Russia!" "That was the best thing that happened to the Vremya program in its half-century history," my former colleague Igor Riskin wrote on Facebook.

On the threshold of a luxurious marble apartment, we are greeted by a slender woman in an elegant tracksuit.

"Tatiana†," she says, introducing herself. "Come in. I live here alone. My son Gosha lives alone. I was the financial director. I invested so much in him, Gosha took English and sports... everything for him alone, and he...."

Tatiana speaks quickly. I can see that she is bored without communication, and she is glad to see me suddenly appear in her house.

"So you were on the air? When I saw it on my iPad, I couldn't believe it...it really looks like a fake," Tatiana continues. "Peskov (Putin's press secretary) called it 'hooliganism.'"

"Well, it's good that it's hooliganism; at least I'm still free." I smile back.

"Yes, Putin is really crazy. He is not right in the head; how could he start this war? Bastards, they even shut down Ekho Moskvy. I used to listen to it all the time. Now I can't watch anything without a VPN. They have blocked everything. Good thing Gosha at least downloaded Telegram and set up opposition channels there.... You should rest; you must be very tired...."

She takes me into a small room and helps me pull out the couch.

When I'm alone, I take a sleeping pill out of my bag, but I can't swallow it. Suddenly I have a severe cough, but I do not feel any symptoms of a cold. I cannot understand what is

† Name changed

happening to me. I almost suffocate. Over time such attacks had become regular occurrences. The cough would come up suddenly in especially stressful situations and would also disappear suddenly.

I fall into a shallow sleep for a while. I wake up early in the morning thinking that I need to start talking to journalists as soon as possible, primarily from Russian media. I have to answer all of their questions so that there will be no more room for conspiracy theories, which were already breeding on the internet at an incredible rate at the time. I need to show everyone that I was not a fake or a project of the secret services but an ordinary person.

I look through a long list of requests from journalists. My gaze rests on the name of the influential Russian edition of *Kommersant*. I write a message saying that I am ready to answer all questions. Just a few minutes later, I get a call. I tell the journalist in detail the reasons for my action. In fact, I recount the same thing I said at the interrogation. Unexpectedly, I get a message from *Kommersant*'s editorial office, saying, "Sorry, we can't publish your interview. We were forbidden."

I remember that the lawyer asked me first of all to contact Ksenia Sobchak. In 2018, she ran for President of the Russian Federation, and then created her own media empire. Her YouTube show has over three million subscribers.

Ksenia opposes the war and wants to come to my house to record an exclusive interview. The repairs in my house are still unfinished and I don't really want to invite journalists to my place, but Ksenia insists. She is interested to see how and with what I live. She says that she is ready to support me and even fly from Turkey to Moscow on the next flight. We stay in touch with her in order to agree on all the details. But after a couple of days, Ksenia Sobchak quietly disappears. [In October 2022, it became known that Sobchak had fled to Lithuania but reappeared in Moscow in November.]

There are no more requests from Russian media. Without wasting a minute, I contact the largest international agency, Reuters.

"Are you going to leave Russia?" they ask.

"No, I am a patriot. I am not going to leave Russia. My family is here and my friends are here. I, of course, understand the scale of the problems that I will have to face, so I am very concerned about my safety."

"Do you consider yourself a hero?"

"No, I don't feel like a hero. I only wish that this sacrifice had not been in vain, and that people's eyes had been opened."

The landlady appears on the threshold of the room as if nothing has happened. "Marina, stop talking and let's go to lunch."

I get up from the computer and go to the kitchen. My thoughts are all over the place. What should I do? I really don't want to emigrate. I have an established life in Moscow. My son is preparing for university, my daughter is in school, and my elderly mother, who lives next door to us, helps me look after the children.

"Gosha was already interested in computers then," Tatiana continues. "He's a boy..."

Her words fly past my ears. I just nod, pretending to listen. The information is hard to absorb.

"You know, my son even accused me in his heart of ruining my whole family's life," I finally join in the conversation. "Today I talked to him for a long time, trying to explain that sometimes you have to do crazy things in life, if only for the sake of making our lives better. He seemed to understand everything."

Tatiana nods understandingly.

I spend the rest of the day talking to foreign journalists online. No one but the lawyers knows where I am. In the evening, I close my eyes and try to sleep again, but a sticky sweat covers my forehead. In my mind, the events of the past few weeks are passing by in a kaleidoscope.

CHAPTER 4

U.S. INTELLIGENCE: THE INVASION WILL TAKE PLACE ON FEBRUARY 16

FEBRUARY 16, 2022, MOSCOW

Accelerate, faster; only seven hundred meters to go. I swim the crawl, the final stage of the training. A little more and I will exceed the distance of five kilometers planned for today. It's noon, and there are only two people in the twenty-five-meter pool. I have to hurry. It's Wednesday; there's snowfall, so there will definitely be traffic jams today. The road to the Ostankino TV Center could take about two hours.

I dry my hair and jump in the car. There's no time for makeup, because in the crazy rhythm of the huge city, every minute counts. I leave the Moscow Ring Road for Kutuzovsky Avenue and get stuck in traffic. My daughter calls.

"Mom, I'm out of school! Are you coming to get me today?"

"No, honey, you forgot. I have a work week. I'm going to work. Our neighbor is picking you up today."

The stream of cars begins to move, and I turn on the radio.

"The alleged Russian invasion of Ukraine that some Western media predicted on the night of February 15–16 did not take place," comes from the speakers. Russian Foreign Ministry spokeswoman Maria Zakharova comments in her Telegram channel: "I ask the U.S. and British disinformation media *Bloomberg*, the *New York Times*, *The Sun*, etc., announce our invasion schedule for the coming year. I would like to plan a vacation."

I switch stations because I don't want to listen to constant trolling from the Russian Foreign Ministry.

"The Echo of Moscow is on the air," the speaker says.

Host: "We have Alexander Kynev, a political scientist, as our guest today on a distant link. Tell me, Navalny's new fraud case is developing right now. I don't know; I've lost count of which fraud case. It's the third one. Is this a time-pressure case?"

Alexander Kynev: "I don't think anyone is surprised by this anymore. It was clear that Alexei Navalny won't get out of jail as long as Vladimir Putin remains president...."

Outside the window, thick snow is falling. Mixed with the reagents that the Moscow authorities generously sprinkle on the streets, it turns into a muddy slurry. A stream of cars slowly creeps into the gray gloom.

My mood is as gloomy as everything around me. Every year the political situation in Russia becomes more and more hopeless. Navalny is in jail; his Anti-Corruption Foundation has been defeated. The authorities are afraid of the "Smart Voting" system, which helped elect opposition-minded candidates. Somehow, imperceptibly, Putin has deprived us of everything: fair elections, independent courts, and the media.

The navigator shows that there is a huge traffic jam ahead; there is a serious accident on the overpass near the Moscow City skyscrapers. I have been stuck in heavy traffic for almost half an hour. I look in the mirror. It's been almost two hours since my workout, but I still have the marks from my swimming goggles under my eyes. Just as I begin to apply my makeup, another message beeps on my phone.

"What do you think the war will start?"

The avatar is Miranda from Sydney. We met her at an international competition in Istanbul. Over a thousand swimmers from all over the world came to Turkey to swim across the legendary Bosporus.

Does my friend from Australia really think a war is about to break out?

"It's impossible," I try to explain to her while I'm stuck in traffic, "there will be no war. Don't worry. Russia and NATO will rattle their arms now and disperse. This is a political bargain. I think that Putin hasn't completely lost his mind."

I drive up to the gate of the TV center. I get out of the car and open the trunk. The policeman carefully checks the license plate with the pass that hangs on the windshield, looks in the trunk. Then he opens the barrier. I park the car and walk quickly to the back of the building. There used to be a concert studio there, but now there is the directorate of Channel One's news programs.

The sleepy policeman at the entrance lazily glances at my working pass. I go up to the third floor, show the pass to Channel One's security officers once again, and go to my workplace.

"How's it going?" I wave to my colleague. But Max does not hear me; he has headphones on his head and he diligently translates something from English. I take off my coat and sit down at the computer. Max finally takes his eyes off the monitor.

"Reuters non-stop shows video of our tanks being brought to the border," he says. "They are being brought in railroad trains. Everyone is fleeing from Kiev. The Americans are urging everyone to leave for Lviv. But we don't show it."

"It's crazy; what does Kiev have to do with it?" I am perplexed. "It's not like they're going to bomb Kiev. Why are the Americans panicking? Now they'll rattle weapons, bargain for more preferences from NATO, and then they'll go away. They will take the equipment back. Putin is not crazy enough to bomb Kiev. The Americans said that the war would start on the night of February 16, but nothing happened; it was just political bargaining. I don't understand why they are evacuating all the embassies in Kiev."

"In today's newscasts we are talking about tanks returning to their permanent locations after training exercises," my colleague reports happily.

"Good news," I say with a smile.

Together we sit in a small office, hung with monitors, and believe in the best. We think the problem is over. On one screen, there is a broadcast of the meeting between Putin and Bolsonaro. On another, Biden speaks. On the other monitors, Russian tanks drive and drive....

CHAPTER 5

WAR IS PUTIN'S FATAL MISTAKE

MONDAY, FEBRUARY 21, 2022

My week off has begun. In the morning, as usual, I walk the dog and take the kids to school. In the car, my hand involuntarily reaches for the radio. I want to turn on the news, but I sharply pull my hand away. After a busy work week, I need an informational detox. And I promised myself that I would spend my first day off without the news.

All day I run around the house, doing the cleaning and cooking dinner. But in the evening I can't stand it. I decide to get out of the information vacuum and go on the Internet. I see the following:

"Members of the Security Council of the Russian Federation supported the proposal of President Vladimir Putin and spoke in favor of recognizing the independence of the Donetsk and Lugansk People's Republics."

I start the video. The frightened voice of Sergey Naryshkin, Director of the Foreign Intelligence Service, comes out of the phone speaker: "Our...Western partners can be given one last chance.... We must otherwise make the decision we are talking about today."

"What do you mean, otherwise?" Putin interrupts him. "Are you suggesting that we start a negotiation process?"

Naryshkin stammers: "I...I...Support the proposal...."

"Endorse or support? Speak up!" insists Putin.

Naryshkin's voice becomes quieter. "I support the proposal to incorporate the Donetsk and Lugansk People's Republics into the Russian Federation," he finally squeezes out.

"We don't talk about it," Putin sneers at him. "We don't discuss it. We're talking about recognizing independence or not."

"Yes," Naryshkin grimly cuts off and leaves the podium.

Everything going on in the Security Council reminds me of some badly staged theatrics. The head of intelligence and the ministers look like terrified rabbits being attacked by a boa constrictor...but they can't even move. I go to bed in a depressed state, anticipating that Russian tanks will again invade the territory of two separatist republics. But the reality is even scarier.

MORNING OF FEBRUARY 24

At 7:00 a.m., the alarm clock on my phone rings. One message after another pops up on the screen.

CNN: "Explosions heard in Kiev."

Meduza: "Russia has launched a full-scale invasion of Ukraine. Putin made an address...."

This is war. No...this can't happen. To bomb Kiev...this is unthinkable; this is madness. PUTIN HAS COMPLETELY LOST HIS MIND. THIS IS A FATAL, HISTORICAL MISTAKE.

I run to the first floor, then back to the second floor. I have to take my son to the subway and my daughter to school. I can't concentrate; my coffee cup falls out of my hands. The shards fly all over the kitchen. The blood pulses in my temples. I grab my phone again and start reading the news.

My mind refuses to believe in the reality of what is happening.

A CNN correspondent in Kharkov reports hearing a series of explosions.

UNIAN reports on explosions near Boryspil Airport. Rocket attacks are carried out in Kiev's suburbs.

CNN writes that explosions are heard in Odesa.

My God, they are bombing Kiev and Odesa. My parents met and married in this beautiful coastal city back in Soviet times in the late 1970s. My father, Vladimir Vladimirovich Tkachuk, was a Ukrainian, a naval officer serving on a warship. Five months after I was born he tragically died in a car accident. All my life I was raised by my Russian mother, a chemical engineer by training, who took me to the Urals to her parents right after my father's death.

With glassy eyes I look at the images on my phone—Russian fighter jets and tanks are flying toward Ukraine. I recall a serene picture from my childhood.

JUNE 1983. USSR, KHMELNITSKY REGION (TERRITORY OF MODERN UKRAINE), CHUVGUZIV VILLAGE.

White huts, buried in the dense foliage of apple trees, could be seen on both sides of the street. My mother and I took an old bus up the dusty road to the very end of the village. The bus stopped at the outskirts. My father's parents' house stood there. We approached a large white hut surrounded by a crumbling wooden fence. An iron mailbox, nailed with a huge nail, dangled from the gate.

I was a five-year-old girl with a short haircut in a white T-shirt, blue shorts, and a white Panama hat. Together with my mother, we walked up to the hut. A hunched-over, skinny old lady came out with a canister in her hand.

"Oh, who came to see us. Maryshenka, what a beautiful girl you've grown to be," my grandmother said in Ukrainian in a loving whisper as she met us at the gate. "Come inside."

My grandmother Ulyana, my father's mother, slowly led us into the house. There were two black and white portraits hanging on the wall. One of them depicted a middle-aged man in a military uniform, my grandfather, who died at the front during World War II. From the second portrait, a young man in a naval officer's uniform looked at me sternly. It was my father. He was the youngest child in a large Ukrainian family, with six other children besides him.

"Your cousin Innochka and Uncle Kolya are there," Grandma said. "They went to the river to catch fish."

Stumbling, I ran through the huge vegetable garden, fully planted with potatoes, toward the river. On the way, I pet a huge white rabbit, munching succulently on grass in a wooden cage.

Almost forty years from now, Russia will launch missile strikes on Ukrainian territory, and Uncle Kolya and Innochka will be hiding in the basement.

Grandmother Ulyana, who went through The Secosnd World War working as a nurse, will not live to see these days. And her children will split in two. The sons would marry and stay in Ukraine, and the daughters would marry and move to Russia. After the war began, the families, who lived on opposite sides of the border, would fall apart for good.

"Why aren't you protesting? Why aren't you taking to the streets to overthrow Putin?" Innochka asks her aunt, who lives in Moscow, over the phone.

"It's not all so clear-cut. Putin knows more than we do. If he made the decision to bomb Ukraine, then that's the right thing to do," her elderly aunt, zombified by Kremlin propaganda, will tell her.

CHAPTER 6

STAY ON THE SIDE OF GOOD

FEBRUARY 28, 2022, DAY 5 OF THE WAR

The work week had begun. Understanding nothing, as if in a fog, I go to the Ostankino TV Center. All entertainment programs are canceled; newscasts are in a continuous stream. The degree of propaganda rhetoric increases with every hour.

Igor Konashenkov, Russian Defense Ministry spokesman, says: "Armed gangs of marauders, looters, and nationalists are rampaging in Kiev.... We must put an end to the endless threats to Russia from the Kiev regime...."

The news anchor reads briskly over the prompter: "The tone is set by President Zelensky. The reason for this is seen by many as a drug addict. You can, for example, assess his behavior, words, facial expressions, gestures. He was grimacing, fixing his hair and constantly wiping his nose. This behavior is common in cocaine addicts."

I feel like a little grain of sand in an ocean of big lies.

On my work monitors are hundreds of thousands of Ukrainian refugees; everywhere there is pain, blood, and children's tears. On my phone there are dozens of messages from all over the world with one single question: "What's going on?" I don't know what to answer. I am hurt, ashamed. I want to disappear from the face of the earth, to die, never to see this again. I have to run away, but my body is chained with fear and my mind is numb. It seems that around me the Devil rules the show.

My boss's loud voice brings me to my senses. He has just returned from another planning meeting. He has a grimace on his face, and a stream of foul language is pouring out of his mouth, as usual. He hates everyone. Since his deputy quit, he has been working like the devil, twelve hours a day, five days a week. He is also sick and tired of the propaganda; he would quit too, but he is warmed by the large sums on his salary card.

He warns us that in times of war we must sit quietly and keep our heads down.

"You are in a warm place. Under war conditions, the Kremlin will only support the army, the security forces, and the propagandists. The rest can go to hell. Let them survive as best they can."

Fear and confusion are on the faces of my colleagues. I notice that all of them are in deep shock from what is happening, but, as they say, "one's own shirt is closer to the body." No one wants to lose their job at such a difficult time.

After midnight, completely exhausted, I go home. There's a new message on the phone. "How are you doing?"

I gasp in surprise. It's from Thomas‡, a well-known British journalist and writer. For more than twenty years he worked

‡ Name changed

in Moscow and wrote several books about Russia. In the midst of the coronavirus pandemic he was taken by ambulance to Sklifosovsky Institute and had emergency surgery. Thomas had no relatives in Moscow. When I found out about the operation, I didn't hesitate for a second and rushed to the hospital to see him.

"We're waiting for the results of the biopsy. We're talking about third- or fourth-degree cancer," the surgeon said in a quiet voice.

"God, it can't be!" Everything inside me shattered.

I wrote long, hopeful messages to his daughter and sister. Every day I drove to the hospital, bringing Thomas the things he needed, the medicine, and taking him to consultations.

"Why do you have to deal with other people's problems? Who are you, Mother Teresa? Don't you have enough problems of your own?" My friends wagged their fingers at me. But I didn't listen to them.

When Thomas got better, he decided to continue his treatment in Great Britain. Early in the morning I drove him to Sheremetyevo Airport for his flight. It turned out to be the last flight to London. Since midnight on December 22, 2020, Russia suspended air links with the UK due to the pandemic. Six months later, Thomas underwent another operation in his home country. Gradually his disease went into remission.

"I've decided to leave Channel One," I write honestly.

"I never understood how such a responsive and sensitive person could work there," Thomas says.

"You know I'm alone. I have two children. I have to feed them. It will be very difficult for me to find a new job. All the opposition media in Russia have been destroyed." I try to justify myself. I feel bitter and disgusted.

"I completely reconsidered my life after I was cured of cancer. Just always stay on the side of good. Stay with light," he writes.

That comment takes my breath away.

CNN shows a destroyed village in the Kiev region. "Man who lost five family members when a Russian missile destroyed his home: 'God, help end this,'" the caption on the screen reads.

"Civilians in Ukraine pay heavy price for Putin's invasion," the host says.

"There was a huge explosion," says a man standing on the ruins of his house, "and we were all buried under the rubble. My twelve-year-old daughter died in a wheelchair, and I and my two grandchildren were pulled out from under the rubble...."

It is impossible to watch. "Stay on the side of good" is going around in my head. At that moment I understood perfectly well what the Ukrainian refugees were going through because I had experienced the same thing as a child.

CHAPTER 7

REFUGEE FROM GROZNY

GROZNY, 1984–1994

I ended up in Chechnya by accident. I was six years old when my mother was invited to head a laboratory at an oil refinery in Grozny. Those were the days of the Soviet Union. There was no Chechnya on the map yet, but there was the Chechen-Ingush Soviet Socialist Republic, where Chechens, Ingush, Russians, Ukrainians, Armenians, and Tatars lived peacefully. There were no nationalist sentiments in Grozny then.

It was a beautiful city, where in summer ripe apricots lay underfoot, and in winter there was almost no snow. My mother liked Grozny very much; she always dreamed of living in the south, so without hesitation she exchanged our apartment in the Urals for an equivalent apartment in Grozny, and we moved.

Together with the boys, I climbed trees, overate ripe mulberries, and rode a bike. In the morning, my mother sent me with a three-liter jar for draft milk. It was usually brought in a huge barrel to a nearby store. Gorbachev had already come to power. Perestroika began in the USSR, which was accompanied by a total deficit. There was almost nothing on the shelves of shops in

Grozny at that time. Therefore, when, in addition to milk, I still managed to buy ice cream for 20 kopecks, my happiness knew no bounds.

A year later I went to school. I was the best in the class. I always tried to be the first in the competitions in the pool. As an excellent student, I was honorably accepted as a pioneer in Grozny's central square. And I was filled with pride.

One could say that it was an ordinary Soviet childhood. Together with my classmates, I carried scrap metal and collected waste paper.

But in the late '90s, when the Soviet Union was already bursting at the seams, my pioneering enthusiasm quickly faded. Imperceptibly, my Chechen classmates began to come to school in headscarves and hijabs instead of red ties. Soviet propaganda constantly imposed atheism on Chechens, but at home children were taught to live according to the laws of the Koran.

I was twelve years old, and I still understood little about religion and politics. But life began to change rapidly. General Dzhokhar Dudayev came to power in the republic. Shortly before the collapse of the Soviet Union, in June 1991, he proclaimed the independent Republic of Ichkeria. Dudayev's supporters seized the building of the Supreme Council, the television center, and the radio house. In fact, from that moment a civil war began in Chechnya. Armed to the teeth, people began to walk around the city.

And on the fence near our school, an inscription suddenly appeared: "Russians—to Ryazan, and Ingush—to Nazran!" Mom often came home in tears. She was not served in the store, but in transport, she was insulted. "Letters of happiness" appeared in our mailbox with anonymous threats to get out of Chechnya.

I will remember the last year in the Grozny school for the rest of my life. With a Chechen girl, I fought in the schoolyard not for life, but for death, to the first blood. I do not remember the reason for our fight. I only remember that everything around us was saturated with hatred and aggression. And neither of us wanted to give up.

I didn't tell my mom about the fight. At some point, she forbade me to go outside. Every day there were reports in the newspapers of numerous murders and kidnappings. More than anything, she was afraid that I might be kidnapped. If we left the house, my mother would ask me to hide my blond hair under a hat or tie a scarf, as the Chechens do. I was a teenager. I was scared, but I did not want to hide anything, and rebelled with all my might.

My indignant tirade was interrupted at some point by a rolling roar. Covering my head with my hands, I instinctively crawled under the table. Suddenly the lights went out and our apartment was plunged into total darkness.

"We must leave here as soon as possible, not today or tomorrow. There will be a full-scale war here," Mom whispered with concern.

She tried to sell our apartment, but no one needed real estate in Grozny.

"In Grozny, they stole weapons from a military unit..." I caught snippets of phrases from the announcer of the Vremya program, coming from the box of a black-and-white TV. Outside the window, the glow from the fire was constantly flickering. Numerous oil wells were burning on the outskirts of the city, and shooting did not stop.

In December 1994, tanks moved on Grozny. Yeltsin decided to restore constitutional order by force in the rebellious republic, which did not obey orders from Moscow. The first Chechen war had begun, which ended with a temporary truce. In 1999, the war continued. According to various estimates, during these years of war, anywhere from fifty thousand to ninety thousand civilians were killed in Chechnya. Hundreds of thousands became refugees.

Abandoning our apartment and all our belongings, we managed to leave Grozny before the full-scale hostilities began. An overcrowded train took us to southern Russia in the Krasnodar region.

"We will give you this lodging for the time you will work in our chemical laboratory," the hostel superintendent said, taking my mother and me to an old barracks on the outskirts of the Kuban village. "There is a fireplace here so you'll need to stock up on firewood. The toilet is in the yard behind that shed, and there is gas for the stove in the gas cylinder. It's better to cook on the stove; that's what everyone here does."

The commandant left, and we were alone in the middle of an empty room. After living in a comfortable apartment, these living conditions were shocking. It was the early nineties when, after the collapse of the Soviet Union, a heady spirit of freedom came to Russia and democratic reforms began. All this was accompanied by uncertainty, lack of money, and unprecedented rampant crime. The new laboratory where my mother had been invited to work never opened. Like millions of other people without jobs, she had no choice but to engage in "shuttle trade." My mother bought huge bales of clothes in Krasnodar, carried them on her back, and resold them at the local market to earn some money for food. An intelligent, weak woman who was not used to commodity-money relations was constantly deceived. There was a catastrophic shortage of money.

"We had dinner tonight for only five rubles," my mother once said happily. "I bought buckwheat and green peas on sale, very cheap."

After such stress she was found to have a cancerous tumor and was operated on. I went to visit her in the hospital, trying to bring her at least some homemade food, as there was no one to help her except me.

As a refugee from Grozny, my classmates at my new school treated me with contempt. As the only refugee in my class, I became an object of constant ridicule and mockery. Kuban had always had a special mentality; they never liked outsiders.

"You belong over there on the last desk, ugly. Don't you dare come near us, you hear me?" said my new classmates.

Biting my lip, I sat down at the last desk. I didn't look good. I was wearing a stretched sweater, on my feet were worn-out boots made of cheap leatherette, and in my hands was a plastic bag, which at that time served as my school bag. But inside of me everything boiled with indignation.

In the morning we could take a bus from our barracks to school, which took the collective farmers to the farm. After school I had to walk home. Every day I would walk about seven kilometers from school to home alone along the dusty country road; sometimes when no one was looking, I cried, cursing the war.

At home I was immediately immersed in the world of books. In a cold, unheated barracks with cracked plaster, I avidly read the books I borrowed from the school library, works by Tolstoy, Gumilev, Solzhenitsyn, Dreiser, Orwell, Kafka, and Remarque, and I memorized poems by Blok, Esenin, Akhmatova, Tsvetaeva, and Bella Akhmadulina. The only person who gave me a ray of hope at that time was a teacher of literature. She just adored me. I could endlessly recite verses and even whole poems in front of the whole class with a special expression.

Mom was in remission. The doctors forbade her to carry heavy bags and she got a job at the local radio. It was then I realized I wanted to be a journalist, help people affected by wars and conflicts and protect all the humiliated and insulted.

In 2000, when I was already working for a regional television station in Krasnodar, I returned to Grozny. A military helicopter with Presidential Envoy Viktor Kazantsev and Chechen head Akhmad Kadyrov flew out of Rostov-on-Don and headed for Grozny. According to the official version, the second Chechen war was over, but there were still shootings and terrorist attacks in Grozny.

A cameraman holding a huge Betacam and I sat in the back of the helicopter. We were the only journalists flying on this flight with officials to Chechnya. I thought with bated breath that in just a few hours, I would be in the city of my childhood.

Flying over the central square of Grozny "Minutka," our military helicopter constantly shot infrared traps. Dozens of luminous rockets flew in different directions; from a distance they looked like fireworks, but in fact they were false thermal targets that protected us from enemy-homing missiles. I tried to make out familiar streets, but all I could see below were grim ruins of houses. We landed near the government quarter. The next day I started asking officials to take us to the Black River District. No one wanted to escort our film crew, as it was dangerous to go there. After a lot of persuasion, they gave us an APC and a group of soldiers. We drove quickly in the direction of my house. I approached the familiar building; our entrance could be seen ahead. A shell hit right in the kitchen, and our whole apartment was turned into a pile of rubble. Next to the collapsed slab, I noticed the headboard of my bed was covered with a thick layer of dust. I couldn't hold back my tears.

"Don't cry. We have to leave; it's dangerous here," my colleague said.

He managed to take a few pictures. People emerged from dilapidated apartments, some of whom I hardly recognized as my former neighbors. For several years now they had been living among the ruins like homeless people, without water, light, and heating. The entire infrastructure of the city was destroyed. In 2003, the United Nations named Grozny the most destroyed city on Earth since the Second World War.

I couldn't get a word out on the way back.

I have hated war ever since. The moment when Russian troops treacherously invaded Ukraine under the cover of night was the point of no return for me. The rebellion in my soul grew with each passing day.

CHAPTER 8

BRITISH SPY OR TRAITOR

MARCH 20, 2022

It is five days after my live protest. I am tired of hiding, so I ask my lawyer to take me home.

The car slowly drives up to the gate of a small cottage community hidden behind a high fence on the outskirts of Moscow. It is late evening. A drowsy security guard reluctantly opens the barrier. We enter a closed territory. Inside this oasis of well-being, there are two hundred new two-story houses, some of which have not yet been completed.

We stop at a low brown fence wrapped in branches of wild grapes. Together with the lawyer, I enter a small two-story house, the walls of which are painted yellow and trimmed with wild stone.

"It's nice here," enthuses the lawyer.

"Yes, it's a paradise for children. There is a forest, a lake, a river, and silence. I put all my strength, all my time and energy into this house. I tried to make sure that my children would have a happy childhood and they would not need anything."

The lawyer leaves. Life seems to be gradually returning to normal. After putting my daughter to bed, I go down to the first floor. My son is in his room studying for his exams. In the kitchen begging for food are two golden retrievers, a mother and her daughter, a playful six-month-old puppy. Her five siblings have gone to different countries. Just for her, I had not yet had time to find an owner. Opening the kennel's website, I try, as usual, to order dog food from the manufacturer. "Your account is blocked." The message pops up on the screen. It must be some kind of mistake, I think.

I pour a glass of wine, cut some cheese, sit down in a chair and try to relax. But the phone is beeping non-stop; there is an endless stream of messages from friends, acquaintances, and foreign journalists. I do not have time to answer. A message from a former colleague of mine pops up on the screen: "Did you see that? They just called you a British spy."

I open the video link that was sent.

"And now for another incident of the week," the familiar Channel One studio and the host, a spectacular blond in a red dress, appear on the screen. "On Monday's Vremya program, a woman with a placard appeared behind the host's back. We paused to look into it. A few words on the matter from my colleague Kirill Kleimenov, Channel One News Chief, who is with me in the studio right now."

Next to the host appears my former boss in a dark suit.

"Of course, that's not why I wanted to appear here in this studio," Kleimenov sadly declares, and once again shows the Channel One audience my anti-war protest live on air. "Within minutes this picture was already in all the major Western media outlets. This is not a metaphor. You can see it yourself. And outside the TV center there was her lawyer. Also in a few minutes. Before that, according to our data, Marina Ovsyannikova had been talking to the British Embassy. Which of you had telephone conversations with a foreign embassy? Not with the visa center, but with the embassy, with its employee, even if he is, as they say, in plain clothes. I, for example, never did. What is my point? No, not spy mania. Let specially trained people do that. My point is to call things by their proper names, and that's all. Emotional impulse is one thing. Betrayal is another. (....) Betrayal is always a personal choice of a person; you can't protect yourself from it, as you know."

Otherwise, if a famous act for thirty pieces of silver had been called "an impulse of the soul," world history would have gone differently.

Channel One's familiar rhetoric about traitors takes my breath away for a second.

At that moment, my son comes down to the kitchen.

"What happened?" he asks.

"You want to laugh, your mom turns out to be a British spy. Kleimenov just said so on the air."

"Ha-ha-ha, let me see," comes the loud bass of my almost two-meter-tall son. "If you were a spy, you'd be the worst spy of our time. You'd blab all the secrets." He laughs heartily.

"Now you understand how propaganda is done on Channel One."

"That's why I never wanted to work on TV."

"I'm very glad you didn't follow in your parents' footsteps and decided to go to medical school. By the way, do you remember that your father and I named you Kirill after Kirill Kleimenov?"

"Yeah, I remember that story. All right, I'm going to bed. I don't have time to listen to the crap that's on TV."

The next day, the British Foreign Office called the statement by Channel One News Chief Kleimenov about my connections to the British embassy a lie: "We have not contacted Ovsyannikova. This is another lie spread by the disinformation machine."

The rhetoric of spies and traitors has been a favorite propaganda device on Channel One. In 2018, after the Skripals' poisoning in Salisbury, Channel One's chief Kirill Kleimenov actually confessed. In a live broadcast, he confirmed that the Kremlin was involved not only in the Skripals' poisoning, but also in several other mysterious deaths of Russian citizens that had taken place on British territory.

"I [...] do not wish anyone to die," Kleimenov said on the air of the Vremya program. "But solely for pedagogical purposes for anyone who dreams of such a career, I would like to issue a warning.... The profession of traitor is one of the most dangerous in the world. Statistically, far more dangerous than a drug mule. Very seldom have those who have chosen it lived in peace and tranquility until their venerable graying years.

"As a future country of residence, do not choose England. There is something wrong there. Maybe it's the climate. But there have been too many strange accidents there in recent years—people hanging themselves, getting poisoned, crashing in helicopters and falling out of windows on an industrial scale."

Silently, like a robot, I would arrive at Channel One, mechanically do my work, and quickly go home, trying to get as little dirty as possible in this filth.

In the morning, together with my lawyer, I went to Ostankino for the last time. We have to pick up my car from the TV center parking lot. Anton enters the closed area of Ostankino; I remain to wait for him outside the gate. A few minutes later my phone rings.

"Do you have a pump in your car?" asks Anton.

"Yes, of course. What happened?"

"You've had all your tires either punctured or deflated. Let me see if I can get it inflated."

"I see. This is petty revenge. Probably one of the policemen was fired after a 'British spy' broke into Ostankino."

Anton laughs out loud. Half an hour later, he drives my SUV out the gate of the TV center.

"I inflated the tires; they don't seem to be flat. You'd better go straight to the car wash and car service. Let them wash it well and look at it thoroughly at the same time. There are all kinds of foreign objects in a car, and bugs can be hidden anywhere there."

"Do you think they know what bugs look like?" I laugh.

When I arrive at the car service, I ask the employee to inspect my car inside and outside to look for foreign objects, especially underbody.

The man is surprised. He scrutinizes the car and finds nothing suspicious. I'm relieved.

The flow of messages on my phone does not stop. Journalists write not only from Europe, but even from Latin America. I have to distract myself or else I'll go crazy, I think, as I drive up to my sports club.

"Give me the key to the gym," I ask the receptionist, holding out my club card.

"Your card is blocked," replies the young man at the reception desk.

With his eyes down to the floor, he says that I am now an undesirable person to them. They have unilaterally terminated our contract.

I have no desire to argue or prove anything, so I turn around and go for a jog along the waterfront.

CHAPTER 9

UNDER THE SUPERVISION OF THE FSB

All of my social media accounts were hacked. While I am trying to regain access to them, a fake page appeared on Instagram with my name and pictures of a woman who looked just like me. Her account is full of new-age swastikas—Z and V symbols, as well as numerous posts in support of the special operation in Ukraine.

It wasn't until ten days after the live protest that I am able to get my Facebook and Instagram accounts back. I start reading personal messages:

"Marina, you gave me back my faith in journalism!"

"It was a breath of fresh air; thank you for the truth."

"Marina, hang in there; we're with you! Take care!"

Next comes a message from an employee of Channel One:

"You forgot to write in your profile header—a common rat. Get treatment in Europe, away from my country. And take your rats with you. Neither you nor they are worthy of this country."

Below is a message from an unknown person:

"Drop dead, traitor!"

At that moment I remember how Yevgenia Albats, editor-in-chief of *The New Times*, asked me during a live broadcast: "Have you thought about what you would say if you were confronted by someone who came up to you and said, 'You spoke out against our president, and Putin called people like you traitors who should be spat out like a gnat out of your mouth'?"

I thought for a second before I answered: "I very much hope that I won't have to face such a person, because there are no such people in my environment. I live in a fairly prosperous place in Moscow. We don't have such an aggressive public here; everyone is thinking and understanding. And even if someone disagrees with my position, I don't think I will receive any threats."

How wrong I was at that moment. The flow of threats from Putin's supporters did not stop. At that moment, when I had already decided to conserve my psyche and not to read the messages on social networks, I see a message from a twenty-four-year-old girl from Samara. Christina, an SMM specialist, offered to help me with social media.

Without thinking twice, I agree, because it is impossible to cope with the flow of information alone. Over time, we become very close, and Christina has become a real lifesaver for me. At any time of day or night, she is ready to help. She knows almost all of my appointments and travels. She writes numerous Google and Twitter requests, sets up two-factor protection on social networks, fights against fake accounts, and even communicates with my lawyers.

"How do you know Christina?" my lawyer Badamshin asks me when I arrive at his office.

"I met her by chance on the internet."

"So? You gave her all your social media passwords?"

"Yes, it helps me a lot."

"Are you crazy? Have you ever seen her? Maybe she's a secret intelligence officer assigned to watch you?"

"I don't think so. She has never let me down yet; for some reason I believe her. I hope my intuition will not let me down."

"Haha," Badamshin laughs. "You believe a woman you've never seen. Well, we'll see, we'll see...."

"Maybe you're the secret intelligence officer?" I joke back.

"Of course, rumors are constantly circulating about me that I work for the FSB."

"I see; we have to keep our eyes and ears open for you. I have a live broadcast with the Italian broadcaster RAI in half an hour."

"Tell them that sanctions are getting in the way of ordinary people's lives."

"Of course, sanctions should be directed at Putin and his entourage, at this gang of criminals who have seized power."

"What is the transmission of the Italians?"

"An evening show, something like our 'Evening Urgent.' I've already started to get on the air. It's going to be live."

The imposing host of *Che tempo che fa*, Fabio Fazio, appears on the screen.

"Good evening. Our guest today is Russian journalist Marina Ovsyannikova, who publicly spoke out against the Russian invasion on live state television."

Once again, I give details of my protest on live television and speak out against Putin, who has unleashed a criminal war.

"Maybe you want to say something important to the people who can hear you now."

"I would like to add one important thing. Many Russians are currently suffering along with Ukrainians. Of course, they are not being shot at or bombed, but Russophobia in the world has reached colossal proportions. You realize that not only the oligarchs are suffering from sanctions, but also ordinary people, especially the middle class, who are oriented toward the West, they are facing this and are rallying around Putin even more. Russophobia causes a backlash in society, so we need to build a dialogue between Russia and Europe. And this dialogue can be built through culture; it is the only way to restore our relationship; it is culture that can unite us."

"Yes, we are all part of the great Russian culture; these days we must reread Dostoyevsky. Thank you again for your courage, Marina." Fazio says goodbye.

The first month of the war was coming to an end. At that time I was sure that Putin was solely to blame for starting the war. A few days later, everything changed. The whole world shuddered when it saw the reports of Russian soldiers' atrocities in Bucha. I read headlines that made my blood run cold:

AFP: "At least 20 bodies seen in one street in town near Kiev."

The Guardian: "Horror in Bucha: Russia accused of torture and massacre of civilians."

This is not just Putin's war. Specific war criminals were operating in Bucha.

"I don't know how we can redeem ourselves to the people of Ukraine," I wrote the next day on my social media. I felt bitter and disgusted.

I really wanted to help Ukrainians, but at that moment I didn't know how I could do it.

A few days later, I came across a message on one of the Telegram channels: "Refugees need clothes and hygiene products." Listed was the address of a sanatorium in Kaluga Oblast, about two hundred kilometers from Moscow.

"Hello, what kind of help do you need?" I asked when I dialed the number.

"We need clothes, shoes, especially children's, and hygiene products. We have a lot of children here. The smallest is a two-month-old baby from Kharkov, many children from two to twelve years old," a woman's voice on the other end of the phone answered.

For several days, my caring friends and neighbors brought things and toys to my house. They carefully put everything together, packed it, and told me what was in which bag.

"These are diapers for a two-month-old baby from Kharkov; these are things for his mom. Just give them all this," a young woman, who had recently become a mother herself, stands on the doorstep.

"Of course I will. Don't worry."

After three days, the first floor of my house is almost completely filled with bags of things. Some man anonymously wired thirty thousand rubles to my bank card as a token of gratitude, so that I could pay the fine. I decided to spend the money to help the refugees, too. There is so much stuff that I had to order a minibus.

The next day, journalists from a major Japanese TV company accompany me to Kaluga Oblast. We met them the day before while recording an interview.

The gates of the camp are closed. There is a guard on duty at the entrance. There are several police officers standing by. We are not allowed to enter the territory of the sanatorium. An elderly grouchy woman in a black sheepskin coat comes out toward us.

"What did you bring? These people don't need much. I'll only take new things. Take the rest to the Red Cross."

"How so?" I ask. "That's not what you told me on the phone. We are journalists. Can we talk to refugees?"

"No. We are closed for quarantine."

Two men in plain clothes are standing next to the car. They are watching the cameraman, who is filming footage of the unloading of humanitarian aid.

"These people look more like hostages than refugees," I say as we get in the car and drive to the Red Cross.

"Yes, they are very carefully guarded. It's unlikely that we can talk to them," agrees the producer from the Japanese TV company.

At that moment, his phone rings. My colleague starts to speak Japanese. I don't understand anything; I just follow his facial expressions. After each new phrase, his face becomes more and more tense and gloomy.

"It looks like we're in trouble," the producer explains. We're going back to Moscow. We can't show this video; we have to destroy it."

"What?! You're crazy! This is the only video of this trip. You can't destroy it! I only managed to take a few pictures. What happened?"

"I just got a call from my boss in Tokyo. They got a call from Moscow and told them not to show anything. Otherwise they would close our Moscow office."

"Are they threatening you?"

"It's just an order from Tokyo. I have to obey. I'm sorry. We're taking a big risk."

"What about freedom of speech? Why do you dance to the Kremlin's tune?"

"There's nothing I can do about it." He looks down. "I'm guessing they figured us out from the license plate of our car. It's registered to our Moscow office."

"What speed! We've been here no more than an hour. And they've already tracked you down and called your office in Japan. Are you sure you can't put that on the air?"

"Absolutely; we don't want to lose our jobs."

"Why don't you give me that video and I'll pass it on to other journalists?"

"I'm sorry, but I can't," he replies.

There is a pervasive silence in the car.

Behind the window of our SUV we quickly glimpse the bare trees. Tired and disappointed, we drive up to the Moscow Ring Road.

CHAPTER 10

JOURNALISM IS A UNIQUE PROFESSION

KRASNODAR, 1996–2002

At first, I was not able to attend university. My test scores were not high enough for me to study for free. Shedding tears, I asked my mother to find money so that I could study at the faculty of journalism, but as refugees, we could not afford it. I spent a year at the preparatory department of Kuban State University, from morning until late at night, preparing for exams. Life had to be put on hold. I didn't have any entertainment at the time. Fortunately, this sacrifice was not in vain, and the next summer my goal was achieved.

"Journalism is a one-of-a-kind profession. If you study journalism and don't write articles or shoot reports, then you're unsuitable for this profession."

I remembered this phrase, uttered by my professor at one of the first lectures, for a long time. I immediately started looking for a job. At first I freelanced, writing articles for the local newspaper and then I did reports for the radio. In my second year, I joined the television station.

It was the main news program of the Krasnodar region. It had an audience of five million people. And the editorial staff was all students. Television became the meaning of our lives. We were ready to work for free. We were literally on fire at work, going from morning to late at night on shoots.

The intensity and variety of the journalism profession suited me perfectly. I didn't need weekends. On Monday I was at a film festival, on Tuesday I was in a cowshed, on Wednesday I met with officials, on Thursday I was in jail doing an interview with a murderer, on Friday I wrote a story about the drought, on Saturday, I wrote about a broken sewer, and on Sunday, I wrote a story about corruption.

It was the beginning of the end of the golden era of modern Russian journalism. There was still a spirit of absolute freedom all around. I wanted to save the people from lawlessness, expose the criminals, and get the city government to repair all the streets. It seemed that by becoming a journalist, I would be able to really work for the public good. But I was very young and naive. The reality turned out to be much harsher.

Late one night, I was sitting in the TV center and was about to go home.

"Marina, there's no one here but you," the editor-in-chief told me. "There's an urgent assignment. We have to go to the airport right now. The head of the Federal Security Service, Vladimir Putin, is arriving there in an hour. We must ask him some questions."

"About what?"

"I don't know. Everything is very secret. There is no information. Ask the purpose of his visit to the Krasnodar region."

"All right. I'll deal with it on the spot."

It was raining, and in the distance we could see the lights of the runway. Together with the cameraman, we were standing in the business lounge of Krasnodar Airport. There were no journalists except for us. Half an hour later, several men in dark suits entered the room. Among them I recognized the recently appointed head of the FSB.

"Good evening, Vladimir Vladimirovich. Tell me the purpose of your visit to the Krasnodar Territory," I asked, holding out the microphone.

"Don't you know the purpose of my visit? What are you even doing here?" Putin replied in an irritated voice. "I've come to appoint a new head of the Federal Security Service for the Krasnodar Territory."

He turned sharply away from the microphone and, accompanied by his guards, walked quickly toward the black limousine waiting for him. I didn't have time to ask him a second question. And I certainly had no idea that I had just met the man who would completely destroy independent media in Russia and then try to change the world order and plunge millions of people into the greatest suffering.

And I certainly didn't suspect that student Margarita Simonyan, who doesn't stand out in anything special at the faculty of journalism and studies a year younger than me, in a few years will head the odious TV channel Russia Today and become one of Putin's main propagandists. After the start of the war, she will call for a nuclear strike on Ukraine.

I first heard about Margarita Simonyan when I was already working on regional television. There was a scandal. As a stringer, she tried to send her material to Moscow, to the TV channel Russia. To do this, it was necessary to go to the territory of our television center. But the director of the Kuban television, Vladimir Runov, did not let her go there. By his standards, Simonyan was quite an ordinary person, not particularly distinguished by either her mental abilities or her external data. She certainly under no circumstances was supposed to get on the federal channel.

But he was deeply mistaken. It was on such nondescript performers from the provinces that the Putin regime at that time made its main bets. It can be said that he was looking for them. There were hundreds of highly educated journalists in Moscow, but suddenly the newly created Russia Today TV channel with a multibillion budget was headed by a particularly unknown twenty-five-year-old journalist from Krasnodar named Margarita Simonyan. It was rumored that her acquaintance with Alexei Gromov from the Presidential Administration and the support of the Armenian diaspora helped her. Whether this is true or just a rumor, I will not say.

However, the fate of Margarita Simonyan at that time did not interest me at all. My career on Krasnodar television was on the upswing. I rose from reporter to presenter of the evening news to deputy editor-in-chief of news. I even had my own authors program. As an independent candidate, I tried to run for the Krasnodar City Duma, but unfortunately, I failed. At that point, I truly admired Putin and wanted to work in the structures of state power. Therefore, I even entered the Department of Information Policy at the Presidential Academy of Public Administration, which was located in Moscow.

But the higher up the career ladder I climbed, the more pressure I felt as a journalist. This became apparent immediately after Vladimir Putin came to power. Federal newscasts began with the president, and regional newscasts began with the governor. In Krasnodar Krai, Alexander Tkachev took the governor's chair.

The phone calls from the regional administration came in a nonstop stream. On the line was the deputy governor, an old friend of the governor's. Previously she had worked in the agro-complex, but now she was giving instructions to journalists: "You should only show Governor Alexander Tkachev. He's meeting with his deputy, then with the cattle breeders. Why didn't you broadcast the governor's trip to the hospital yesterday? How come you didn't have time to edit it? Why?"

"We just didn't make it in time," my boss replied. "Yesterday there was a big accident with a passenger bus; a lot of people died there. That was the big news."

"The big news is the governor!" shouted the official on the other end of the line.

At some point my eyes opened. I realized that I no longer wanted to serve the interests of petty officials. Young journalists were trying to get out of the stuffy atmosphere of the provinces and went to Moscow. I wanted to go there too, but I lacked determination. Then a chance came when the management of our television company changed.

"You won't be anchoring the news anymore and your program will be closed," the new boss, a middle-aged blond with lush, curly hair, told me with distaste in her voice.

"Without thinking, I took a piece of paper and wrote my resignation letter. A few days later, after dropping everything in Krasnodar, I was already flying to Moscow. I had to start my life all over again. I only had vague promises from friends to help me get a job in television. I had two months' worth of money left on my bank card.

CHAPTER 11

A PRIVATE CLUB FOR THE ELITE

MOSCOW, 2002–2021

Moscow greeted me with a piercing cold wind. As soon as I got off the plane, terrorists seized the Dubrovka Theater Center and demanded the withdrawal of troops from Chechnya. They held more than nine hundred people hostage. For the next three days, the entire country sat in front of the television. One live feed was succeeded by another.

"Come home soon," my mother called me in terror. But I was determined, and I had no intention of backing down. I rented a room on the outskirts of the city and started looking for a job.

Once again I had to go through all the circles of hell. First, I had to work freelance for a newspaper, then for an advertising agency, and then a sports TV channel.

"Come over tonight; we'll try you as an editor. You know how to write headlines, don't you?"

My new acquaintance from Ostankino was the head news editor at Channel One. I couldn't believe my happiness. It had been my most cherished dream to work at Channel One, but it was impossible to get there from the street without patronage.

"You know, it's a private club," he explained. "Somebody's friends and kids and wives work there. Even if they take you for an internship, it's not certain that at the end you'll be offered a contract. You might work for free for a few months, and then bye-bye. Another free intern will be hired in your place."

But I was willing to do anything. In the morning I ran to take a session at the Presidential Academy, and in the evening I rushed to the Ostankino TV center. The temporary paper pass I presented at the entrance was proof of my belonging to a special caste.

For almost four months I worked for free. From 7:00 p.m. to 3:00 a.m., I transcribed news agency reports, processed press releases, and summarized all the reports. The presenter would then read all this on the air to the Far East and Siberia. In Moscow it was the middle of the night, but there it was already daytime. All the newcomers were first tried out on these regional broadcasts, which were always considered secondary.

It was the war, which I hated so much, that got me into the "inner circle." In March 2003, American troops invaded Iraq. The occasion was the George W. Bush administration's claim that Saddam Hussein had weapons of mass destruction and that his regime was therefore a serious threat. In order to convince the waverers, U.S. Secretary of State Colin Powell demonstrated a test tube with anthrax spores on the UN podium. True, a year later he admitted that no stockpiles of weapons of mass destruction actually existed in Iraq. The information provided to him by the CIA was wrong. The pretext for military aggression was far-fetched.

After the American invasion of Iraq, Channel One urgently needed people with English skills. I had to watch CNN and Al-Jazeera, which reported the latest news on the fighting. I was finally offered a contract, which, however, had to be renewed every month.

After another six months, I was officially on the staff of Channel One with a permanent salary. It seemed that the dark streak in my life was over; finally, I became a full-fledged member of this club for a select few.

I remember how, on the first day, I walked with bated breath into the main newsroom. It was a large space with huge windows and lots of computers, and in the middle of it stood a long table. Behind this desk a production team was getting ready to go on the air. A few people were concentrating on the layout of the program, distributing the cameras in the studio, and checking the tape numbers. At both ends of the room, behind glass partitions, sat the presenters. On the right was daytime news anchor Zhanna Agalakova. On the left was Ekaterina Andreeva, the presenter of the Vremya program. They were the stars of the channel. They seemed like celestials to me.

At the time, I could not even imagine how unexpectedly and strangely our paths in life would intertwine. Andreeva would become the face of Putin's propaganda, for which several countries would impose personal sanctions on her. I would shout anti-war slogans on her airwaves, and she would continue to pretend that nothing was going on. (Although later she would say that she agreed with the anti-war slogans on my poster.)

Agalakova would soon leave the anchorwoman's chair, feeling the beginning of information pressure, and go to Paris as a foreign correspondent. With the outbreak of war, she would resign from Channel One and give up all state awards in protest. She would send her medals by parcel post to the Kremlin with a note: "*Mr. President, your leadership leads the country to the abyss. I find your awards unacceptable.*" It was Zhanna who would connect me with the people who would help me, but more on that later.

The news hive was buzzing. I sat at my computer, painfully choosing words to summarize the story. It seemed to me that the country's main TV channel needed to be written in a special way.

"Everyone writes as they breathe," Jeanne said, interrupting my agony. By rearranging a couple of sentences and replacing a few words, she instantly made the text light and clear. It was just under twenty minutes until the 3:00 p.m. newscast.

"Where's the text about the fire festival in Spain? I need it right away." A short guy with big blue eyes was standing behind me. He was visibly embarrassed when I turned around.

Igor was twenty-three years old and an assistant director. He was brought to Channel One by his mother, who also worked there as a production editor. Despite the fact that he was an "insider," he also had to do a long internship to get into this closed club.

Igor took me under his wing. He introduced me to his colleagues, and during breaks we went to lunch at a café near the TV center. Then we started meeting with his friends outside the office. Somehow it just happened that we became a couple. A year after we met, we got married and had a son.

"Let's call him Kirill, after the best presenter of the program *Time*, Kirill Kleimenov," I suggested.

"Great idea. I like that name," my husband agreed.

Next to me in the crib, wrapped in a bundle of diapers, a little newborn was sleeping soundly.

At the end of 2012, in response to U.S. sanctions, the State Duma decided to ban Americans from adopting Russian children. It was popularly called "The Scoundrel's Law." Two hundred and fifty-nine children, mostly with developmental disabilities, who were already ready to fly out to their adoptive parents in the United States, remained in Russia forever. The lives of most of them could have been made much easier with the help of technology that was unavailable or inaccessible to these orphans in Russia. Adoption of the disabled in our country is very difficult. These children were doomed to spend their entire lives in state-run orphanages. It was tantamount to prison.

"How can they do such a ruthless thing?!" I was indignant.

"Putin is doing everything right. Our children should stay in Russia," Igor answered.

His career was on the rise. Since we got married, he had changed several state television companies and in recent years worked in the top management of the Russia Today television channel. Margarita Simonyan, whom I knew from Krasnodar, became his boss.

By that time, we already had a daughter. Our family roles were divided thus: he earned money and built his career, while I took care of the family and the kids. I worked on a comfortable schedule. I wanted a quieter life, without business trips.

Leaving my tiny apartment in the suburbs of Moscow, we took out a mortgage and moved first to a two-room apartment on the outskirts of Moscow and then to a three-room apartment. But after the sharp rise in the exchange rate, we could not afford a loan. The prospect of becoming homeless loomed. I decided to act. We sold the apartment, paid off the mortgage, and used the remaining money to buy a small plot of land.

I decided I could build a house on my own. Money was tight, and the task was incredibly difficult. To save money, I turned into a foreman for a few years. Each of my days off started with buying building materials and studying utilities, and ended, as a rule, with a quarrel with the builders who had once again forgotten to dig a trench and put insulation.

Two years later, our agony was over and we finally moved out of the temporary housing and into our own house. The interior was still unfinished and the heating didn't work, but I was still overwhelmed with pride. The ambitious project was complete. We had gotten rid of the mortgage, and our children would grow up away from the bustling metropolis.

Igor arranged books on the shelves in his room, most of which were opuses by the ideologue of the "Russian world" by Alexander Dugin. At first I didn't pay much attention to it, but over time, propaganda began to corrode our family relationship like rust. At home we would try not to talk about politics, but when we came to visit our friends we would argue to the point of grief.

"Instead of taking care of our citizens, the Kremlin spends a lot of money on brainwashing," I told my husband. "I don't want our taxes to fund *Russia Today*. You are zombifying foreigners."

"We work in the interests of the country," Igor argued hotly. "Putin is a great geopolitician; he thinks globally. And television is an instrument of propaganda everywhere. You think there's no propaganda in America?"

"Yes, but in America there is Fox News along with CNN, and you can always change the channel, compare, analyze. And in Great Britain there is the BBC, an independent television company, whose work is paid for by the viewers themselves with an annual subscription. In our country, all the channels blow the same horn, because they are all controlled by the Kremlin."

"You don't understand anything. Putin is reviving the empire that Gorbachev destroyed. He is defending the interests of the Russians, the annexation of Crimea will go down in history. It's the best thing Putin has done," Igor said.

I replied, "He simply brazenly snatched the peninsula from Ukraine, ignoring international law."

After such arguments we could not talk for hours. Each of us would stick to our own opinion. At some point we realized there was nothing left to talk about. Our relationship was completely exhausted, and we parted ways.

Immediately afterward, all *Russia Today* employees were required to sign a non-disclosure agreement. They were forbidden to discuss what was going on at the channel with outsiders, or to criticize *Russia Today* on social networks. This agreement is valid for twenty years after their dismissal. If they violate it, they will have to pay a multimillion-dollar fine.

Our divorce was quite civilized. I stayed with the children in the house that I had worked so hard to build. Igor wasn't interested in the house at all. He took his car and moved into his apartment in Moscow. His salary by that time was three times higher than mine, and he valued his job and his status very much. I thought he was locked in a golden cage, and after the war began, he quietly sold his soul to the devil.

CHAPTER 12

PROPAGANDA FACTORY

After my divorce, I slowly drifted downstream. Working at Channel One had long ceased to arouse the same awe, but rather a persistent aversion. There were fewer and fewer professionals in the newsroom, and more and more vacancies. Like hundreds of my colleagues, I silently observed all the degenerative processes.

For many years, Channel One has had such a concept as *obyazon* (**the absolute priority**). It is a video that must be given in the news. In the beginning, these were stories that the channel's management was interested in, for example, premieres of films produced by the channel or fashion shows.

But gradually, all the videos that were sent to us from the Kremlin became obyazon. When the president did not want to go out in public for a long time, we were sent canned food. There were pre-prepared meetings of Putin with officials. We put them on the air so that people would not worry about the president's long absence.

In 2007, before the presidential election, the number of obyazons increased dramatically. The Kremlin ordered all newscasts to begin with stories about Dmitry Medvedev. It became clear that Putin had found a clever way to bypass the Constitution, which did not allow him to hold the highest office for more than two consecutive terms, and to fool his own people. He chose his interim successor, and Russia took another step toward the abyss.

Film crews followed Medvedev around the clock, recording his every move. His meetings were frankly boring, but no one talked about the obyazons from the Kremlin. The so-called "news" about Medvedev and Putin occupied almost every newscast at the time. There was no time left to show Russians the really important events that were happening in the country and the world. Editors-in-chief were careful to watch the wording used by correspondents. Any wrong word said on air about Putin or Medvedev was punishable by a fine. The fine was sometimes as high as 40 percent of the monthly or weekly salary. In the event of a serious mistake, employees were immediately fired. There were no irreplaceable people in that propaganda factory.

Stories went through several stages of filtering. First they were proofread by ordinary editors, then by chief editors. If it was a particularly important story, the edits were made personally by the head of the Directorate of Information Programs, Kirill Kleimenov.

There was a strict ban in the editorial office—no bad news could be placed after the stories about Putin. There could be no negative information next to the president's name. From year to year, state television has molded Putin into the savior of the Russian land. In the case of any negative events, the idea was constantly broadcast that the tsar was the good one, he was just not aware of what was happening, and the boyars (tsar's servants) were the bad ones. Only they were to blame for everything.

In the international newsroom where I worked, there was even a tacit ban on good news from the U.S. and Western Europe. In the minds of Russians, there had to be an image that all Americans were LGBT supporters who killed black people and abused adopted children from Russia. Even such an event as the annual Academy Awards was banned.

For several years, my workday began with listening to briefings by U.S. State Department official Jennifer Psaki. At some point on Russian television she became a favorite punching bag. Channel One mocked Psaki in a particularly sophisticated way. The Russian propaganda was played along by APTN journalist Matthew Lee, who constantly asked Psaki qualifying questions. On May 12, 2014, wearing headphones, I listened to their dialogue about illegal referendums in Ukraine.

Jen Psaki: We do not recognize the illegal referendum that took place in parts of the Donetsk and Luhansk regions last weekend. It was illegal under Ukrainian law and was an attempt to cause further division and disorder in the country. Its technique was also highly suspicious because of reports of electoral carousels, pre-marked ballots, children voting, voting for absentees and even voting at polling stations in Moscow and St. Petersburg.

Matt Lee: Sorry, I might just be in the dark and trying to guess what this is: "electoral carousel." What is it?

Psaki: Honestly, I read that, but I'm also not familiar with the term. It probably means that people didn't register when they voted. I'll check and find out what our team of experts meant by the term.

Lee: Since there was talk of children voting, doesn't that mean they were sitting on horses moving in circles?

Psaki: I don't think that was implied, Matt.

Having made a full transcript of this dialogue, I brought it to the editor-in-chief's office.

"We take out these words about the illegal referendum. We leave the 'merry-go-rounds' and the part of the dialogue where Matthew is trolling Psaki," said the editor-in-chief, completely crossing out Psaki's words, which did not fit our propaganda rhetoric.

Before the U.S. election, we deliberately began to exalt Donald Trump and mock Hillary Clinton. When she collapsed at the 9/11 ceremony, the incident was "remembered" for a week. She was generally sought to be portrayed as sick, self-serving, and extremely mean to Russia. The same tactics were used in the next election against Joe Biden.

In the new information reality, it was not news that mattered, but "the right commentary." There was a real hunt for people in the West who would broadcast the Kremlin's point of view. The "right" American and European political analysts were worth their weight in gold for us. These people were few in number, and so the producers' staff kept their phone numbers. Everyone played by the carefully circumscribed rules. No outsiders ever appeared on the air of the Kremlin's main mouthpiece. Lists of people invited to the airwaves were known in advance. During the recording of the online interviews, I asked the "right" questions and invariably got the "right" answers. If it was impossible to get the right video commentary, I used quotes from newspapers.

"I am so sick of all this," my immediate superior wailed after almost every broadcast. During the newscasts, we began to turn off the sound and defiantly turned away from the TV.

In general, my colleagues on state television could be divided into two parts—ideological ones. There were those who really supported Putin, but very few of them. Most, of course, were simply cynical and worked for good money. In the morning they anonymously signed petitions in defense of democracy, and in the evening they made stories about the rotten West.

The Channel One News Directorate was especially perplexed after Alexei Navalny returned to Russia from Germany. The Kremlin denied any involvement in his Novichok poisoning until the very last moment. But Navalny himself found his FSB assassin, called him, and the assassin confessed to everything.

On January 17, 2021, a plane with an opposition politician landed in Moscow, and he was immediately arrested. While the internet was buzzing, the Vremya program was silent. Only on January 23, 2021, did Vremya host Ekaterina Andreeva tell viewers that Navalny could face new criminal charges for calling illegal rallies. The opposition leader was not even shown on Vremya. The practice of silencing important news on state television has become a regular occurrence.

"This is already beyond good and evil. The cynicism is simply outrageous," I said to my immediate boss.

He nodded sadly in response. A few months later, after saying goodbye to everyone, he said, "I can't take it anymore!" and left. He had worked at Channel One all his life. He didn't have much time left before his well-deserved retirement.

CHAPTER 13

NEW JOB

APRIL 2022

"Dear Marina," I read the message from a German number. "My name is Jaka Bizilj. I am the head of the Cinema for Peace Foundation. Can you join us tomorrow for a live broadcast on Welt TV?"

"Jaka Bizilj, what a familiar name," I think, remembering that he had helped evacuate Navalny when he was poisoned with Novichok. "Thanks for the invitation. Of course, I'll go on the air with you. Only I sometimes have problems with the internet," I reply.

We discuss the technical details of the inclusion over the phone.

The next day, Jaka sends me a message again: "Media Concern Axel Springer wants to hire you. Would you like to work with the newspaper *Bild* or *Welt*?"

"I would have preferred *Welt*," I reply. As far as I understood at the time, *Welt* is the equivalent of the Russian *Kommersant*.

A few days later we sign a contract for my freelance work with a fixed salary. We did not discuss any more details at that point.

Representatives of the publishing house Axel Springer issue a press release. "Marina Ovsyannikova will become a freelance correspondent of *Die Welt*, covering events in Ukraine and Russia. At the crucial moment, Marina Ovsyannikova had the courage to present an unvarnished look at reality to Russian viewers. Despite the threat of state persecution, she defended an important part of journalistic ethics. I am very happy to work with her," Ulf Poshardt, editor-in-chief of the Welt Group, wrote.

My new colleagues contact me, and soon the paper publishes my first article, titled "Russians Are Afraid." In it, I question the sociological research of the Levada Center, which polled more than 80 percent of Russians who supported Putin.

"The survey was conducted under conditions of dictatorship. In the midst of war, when any word against it is considered treason. And for that they put you in jail for ten years. Russians are frightened. In Moscow, almost no one picks up the phone when someone else's number rings. Young people in megalopolises don't participate much in polls. As a rule, they involve a lot of older people who live in rural areas."

"I have a brilliant idea," I write to my new boss from the international department, *Die Welt*, the next day. "You said that I would cover events in both Russia and Ukraine. I want to go to Kiev as an independent journalist. I will make stories about war crimes in Bucha, about the shelling of Odesa. I can work together with international experts. Maybe we will manage to record an interview with Zelensky."

"Are you sure you want to go to Ukraine? It's very dangerous. Come on; you'd better come to Berlin. You'll meet everybody."

"I'm sure I really want to go to Ukraine. I'm a journalist. But I need a Schengen visa. My previous visa expired during the pandemic."

"It's not a problem. You have to wait a week, and we'll resolve the issue. You can go through Poland or through Latvia," my boss replies.

"I don't want to wait. Every minute is precious to us. We have to do something to stop this bloodshed. I know a way to get into Ukraine without a visa, through Moldova."

"That's a great idea. I'll have to talk to the management about it."

Another few days are spent coordinating all the details of the trip.

It's mid-April, and the snow has almost melted, but the spring sun is not warm at all. I run around the house and throw warm clothes into my suitcase.

"Where are you going again?" my son asks.

"I'm going on a work trip for a couple of weeks, a month at the most. I won't be available for a few days for security reasons. I won't be able to return your calls. I hope you can handle it. I told your grandmother she'll help you."

"We don't need any help," my son answers in a business-like manner. "We're not little; we'll figure it out on our own. By the way, did you see how many memes appeared on the internet after your protest?"

"No, I haven't. Show me."

He shows me some posters in the Channel One studio, with funny inscriptions. Together we laugh out loud. I am glad that the children are trying to take the difficult situation our family finds itself in in a humorous way.

"Where are you going?" my daughter asks.

"To Germany, honey. I'll work for a while and come back," I say with my eyes down.

"I saw on the internet that *Welt* offered you a job."

"You know everything, but you don't fly," I say, deliberately cheerful, trying to lighten the mood.

My daughter looks at me inquisitively, as if she's trying to guess something. Her huge blue eyes are filled with fear.

I can't tell the children the truth that I'm going to war. It's very dangerous. I don't know what awaits me in burning Ukraine. What if I don't come home? What if we accidentally come under fire? Should I take that risk? Should I fly to Germany in peace? Doubts gnaw at me all night.

In the end, my professional duty as a journalist is stronger than my fear. I decide to go to Ukraine. In the morning, after buying groceries and leaving money for the children, I call a cab and drive to Vnukovo Airport.

"Dear passengers, the check-in for the flight from Moscow to Istanbul is over. The boarding for the flight to Yerevan has started," the loudspeaker announces.

With my large suitcase, I run through the half-empty hall of Vnukovo Airport. There are few passengers in my way. Since the start of the war and the imposition of sanctions, almost all foreign flights have been canceled. The only way to get to the European Union from Moscow is to change planes via Serbia, Armenia, or Turkey.

My burgundy suitcase slowly creeps along the luggage belt. I pick up two boarding passes to Chisinau with a connecting flight to Istanbul. I walk toward passport control.

After scanning it, the border guard looks up at me in surprise.

"Step aside. You are about to be approached."

After a few minutes, a man in plain clothes asks me, "Where are you flying to, Marina Vladimirovna?"

"To Istanbul. I need to rest. The events of the last few weeks have been too stressful. I'm late for my flight."

"You'll make it; your flight is delayed." The man is in no hurry to finish the conversation. "And where will you rest? What hotel?"

"I'm not staying in a hotel but at a friend's." I remembered that an acquaintance of mine left Moscow in a hurry after the war began and temporarily settled in Istanbul.

"Well, well," he says with distrust. "And you're flying alone? Without children?"

"Alone. The children stayed with their grandmother. They have school now."

"All right, sit here."

"I can't wait any longer; the flight will be boarding soon."

Without saying anything else, the man leaves. At that moment, a loudspeaker announces that the flight to Istanbul has been delayed for technical reasons.

I calm down. I take out my phone and call Badamshin, my lawyer.

"Tell me, what should I do? They won't let me out. I'm afraid I'll miss my flight."

"Don't worry. I think they'll let you go now. That's the way they always check you before you leave. Get used to it."

After twenty minutes, two more men come up to me. They start asking the same questions a second time. I patiently answer. An hour later they hand me my passport. Only because of the technical delay of the flight do I make it to the plane.

"Our plane has landed in Istanbul," the stewardess announces cheerfully.

I grab a small bag from the overhead bin and turn on my phone. A message from ***Welt*** pops up on the display: "Peter[§]

§ Name changed

will be waiting for you at the hotel in Chisinau. He is our security advisor."

After that, they send me personal information and a picture of Peter. I understand that he is British. I am surprised, but I do not ask unnecessary questions.

Next comes another message: "Turn off your phone and take out the SIM card. They won't be able to track you. They'll think you're in Istanbul."

I promise to do this after I get on the plane. The huge "Transfer flights" display shows the nearest flights. I see my flight to Chisinau and run to another part of the transfer terminal.

At that time, information that I had left Moscow had already appeared on the internet. The intelligence services instantly published the flight and time of my departure, accompanying the messages with sarcastic comments.

"The scandalous journalist Marina Ovsyannikova took the 12:40 flight from Vnukovo to Istanbul today. Most likely she went abroad for permanent residence. Ovsyannikova's provocation itself was necessary in order to gain fame and beg foreign handlers for favorable terms of employment in some Western publication engaged in anti-Russian propaganda.

"We have to assume that if Ovsyannikova does go back to Russia, it means she will do so after receiving some kind of assignment from her Western handlers. According to unofficial information, one of these handlers' 'friends' is a journalist accredited to the Russian Foreign Ministry, who, incidentally, is a British citizen."

Reading these reports, I realized that the intelligence officers had hacked into my phone. I was so naïve that I hadn't even cleaned my contact list before I started protesting. My list contained phone numbers from the U.S., Great Britain, and other NATO countries. Working in an international newsroom, I was in constant contact with foreigners. Thinking that now all my acquaintances from around the world could be called "handlers" and "spies," I was horrified and immediately started sending out messages from the Istanbul Airport, warning everyone that my phone had been hacked.

Twenty minutes remain before the flight to Chisinau leaves. Before I pull out my SIM card and disappear for good, I have to send a few dozen messages. Most importantly, I have to warn Thomas not to return to Russia under any circumstances. If unofficial sources write that the British journalist is my "handler," this is a hint that he will be arrested right at the airport.

Throughout the flight, I painfully ponder this possibility. I am terribly ashamed that I accidentally dragged innocent people into this story.

The rare lights of the airport flicker outside the window. Late at night, a Turkish Airlines plane lands at Chisinau International Airport.

I hold out my red passport to the officer.

"Come this way," the uniformed officer calls me aside. "What is the purpose of your visit to Moldova?"

"I am a journalist for the German newspaper *Die Welt*. I am on a business trip."

I hand him the supporting documents. But that is not enough. There is a war nearby, and people in Moldova are not inclined to trust the word of people with Russian passports. I understand this reaction, so I do not ask unnecessary questions. I sit tiredly on the bench and wait.

The passport control area gradually empties out. About an hour goes by, and the officer finally hands me my documents.

"You can go." He smiles.

"Fine," I take my passport back, happy that all the misunderstandings are over.

CHAPTER 14

INFORMATION WARFARE

CHISINAU, MOLDOVA, APRIL 2022

Under cover of night, I take a cab to a small hotel on the outskirts of Chisinau. A tall man of athletic build comes out to meet me.

"Peter?" I ask cautiously.

"Yes. I am waiting for you," the stranger answers in a low voice and heads in the direction of the hotel. I pick up my suitcase and follow him.

We enter the elevator. In the light of the dim lamp, I scrutinize Peter's stern face. Here he is, a real British intelligence agent. He must have been specially sent to meet me. Why is a German newspaper collaborating with the British? My God, is all this happening to me in real life and not in a dream? More and more questions, for which I find no answers, keep popping up in my head. But I don't ask them; I just observe the mysterious stranger in silence.

Peter goes to the door of the room and opens the lock with the electronic key. Before going inside, he looks around carefully. There is no one else in the hallway but us.

"Do you think we're being watched?" I ask carefully.

"I have to check everything. I was told that I would have a special secret client."

Peter goes to the window, pulls back the heavy curtains, and looks out into the distance. It's pitch black outside, with only a few lonely street lamps burning.

After typing in the electronic code, I try to open my suitcase, but the lock seems to be jammed. That's all I need. Peter is still standing by the window, watching me carefully. His gaze makes me uncomfortable.

"If you're afraid, I can stay here," the security guard suddenly suggests.

"No, thank you. I'm not afraid. It's just that I'm very tired and want to sleep."

Peter nods, turns around, and walks to the door.

"If you need anything, I'm in the room across the hall. I still have to write my evening report," he says.

"Evening? It's the middle of the night," I say, trying to lighten the mood.

But Peter is not inclined to joke. Tilting his short-cropped head, he leaves without saying anything. The red LED of the electronic lock flashes on the door. Just in case, I close the door with an extra latch. After several attempts I manage to open my suitcase. After taking a shower, I fall into a deep sleep, feeling like the hero of some spy detective movie.

In the morning I meet Peter for breakfast in the hotel's little restaurant. I take a cup of coffee, sit at the farthest table, and take my time looking at the guests. The closest to us are two women in their fifties, talking passionately about something in Moldovan. A little farther away from them, a lonely man, in jeans and a gray sweater, is finishing his morning coffee and a sandwich.

Next to the table are three journalists from some foreign TV channel. One of them is wearing a khaki vest with many pockets. His long hair is tied up in a ponytail. Under the table there is a professional video camera.

"...today in Ukraine," I hear a fragment of his phrase.

A little farther away is a family with two young children. A three-year-old boy is excitedly tossing lettuce leaves from his plate.

"What are you doing?" Indignant, the young woman asks him in Ukrainian and moves her plate to the other side of the table.

Everything looks quite mundane, nothing suspicious.

Peter eats his second omelet and sandwich with gusto.

After eating, he whispers to me that after breakfast we will need to change hotels for safety reasons. He also says that I'll need to buy a new phone, a local SIM card, and create a new Google account.

"Okay. I'll ask Christina to help me set it up," I agree.

"Christina? Who's that?"

"My assistant. She is the only person from Russia who knows that I am in Moldova now."

"Where did you meet her?"

"Online. She offered me her help with social media."

"Are you an idiot? Do you really trust her? Maybe she's FSB? Tell her to send her passport, and I'll check it out."

"Maybe you work for the British secret service? Who do you write the evening reports to?"

Peter laughs. "It's much simpler than that. To protect journalists, a German media concern contracts with a British security firm because its employees have combat experience. I served in Iraq and Afghanistan."

I raise my eyebrows in surprise. Peter clearly doesn't look like an ordinary soldier. I continue to listen to him.

"Two weeks ago I worked with a journalist from *Bild*. He decided to do a report from the suburbs of Kharkiv. I told him not to go there; it was dangerous. But he didn't listen to me. In the end, we approached the village. And we ran into the Russians; they were only two blocks away. The shooting started, and I kicked the gas and ran out of there. There was a female translator from Kiev with us. She was so scared she couldn't say a word. The next day she refused to work with us. We were left without an interpreter. But I speak a little bit of Ukrainian myself."

"Where did you learn it?" I ask, puzzled.

"My wife is from Zaporizhzhya."

"How interesting! Where did you meet her?"

"In Turkey, in a hotel. We lived in Kiev for a while, and now we live in Budapest. My son was born six months ago," Peter says, and his stern face softens with a smile for the first time.

After breakfast, we get into a car with Polish plates, which Peter had rented in Warsaw, and drive to another hotel. The car winds its way through the narrow streets of Chisinau. Behind the window we see trees with fresh green foliage. Lonely passersby leisurely go about their business.

"Why does the car smell so badly of gasoline?" I ask, opening my window to air out the interior.

"We have two huge cans of gasoline in the trunk. It's impossible to buy fuel in Ukraine," the security guard explains.

We stop at a traffic light. Peter looks at his phone. "Did you see that a Ukrainian missile just hit the cruiser Moskva? Does it look like it's going down?"

"There must have been conscripts there," I say. "The Russian Ministry of Defense lies to the mothers all the time. In the first days of the war they said that there were no conscripts in the war. But in early March, after the Ukrainians captured several conscripts, the Russian Defense Ministry was forced to admit that they were there. The exact numbers are unknown. I'm used to Russian authorities lying all the time. In mid-February, Putin said, we will not attack Ukraine; a few days later the war started. And so all the time, 'We weren't there,' 'It wasn't us.' Frankly, it's disgusting to listen to all this."

I continue, "I can't wait for us to get to Kiev. Then I can tell the Russians that this is a real war, a despicable and criminal one. This is not a special military operation to liberate Donbass, as Putin says it is."

"Putin is destroying his own people. He is destroying Ukraine; he is destroying Russia. He is weakening Europe. There are millions of refugees everywhere; we have gasoline supply difficulties. Who do you think benefits from this whole situation?" Peter looks at me meaningfully. "America! Of course, only America."

"Yes, you're absolutely right," I nod, knowing full well that the war is destroying the economies of all European countries. They are forced to buy expensive shale oil and liquefied gas from the United States.

We pull into the parking lot of a small hotel, leave our things in our rooms, and go into town to get a new phone. As soon as I get off the phone, an official letter arrives from the publication's editors.

"Marina Ovsyannikova is a freelance correspondent for ***Welt***. She will be covering events in Ukraine," reads the text. Below is a message saying that we can go to Kiev tomorrow morning.

I show the letter to Peter.

"They've gone crazy there in Berlin," said the experienced security guard. "You need official accreditation. This is a war zone. And you have a Russian passport. They'll arrest you at the first checkpoint. I'm not going anywhere. We need accreditation from the Ukrainian government and someone to meet us at the border and take us to Kiev."

"I agree; it is very dangerous to go to Kiev without official permission from the Ukrainian authorities. My colleagues in Berlin suggest that we wait a few more days. They promise that in the near future they will contact influential people from Ukraine and resolve all organizational issues."

Back in my room, I start looking through the news feed, trying to understand what is happening in Ukraine right now. Suddenly my eyes stop on a message: "Dozens of young Ukrainians, waving yellow and blue flags, came to the *Welt* newspaper office in Berlin. They shouted 'Ovsyannikova, geet!' protesting her employment.

"Ukrainians said that the journalist was a Kremlin project designed to destabilize the situation. Representatives of the newspaper came out to the protesters. They explained that they would not turn their backs on this woman because she was 'on the right side of history.'"

What is going on? Why are they protesting? I don't understand. I open the Ukrainian media and read: "Not all Ukrainians believed in the sincerity of the anti-war performance on Russian TV."

"This incident is a production; there are no live broadcasts in Russia."

"The demonstration of the opposition inscription is nothing less than 'another act of the Russian Federation's hybrid warfare against Ukraine.'"

"Ovsyannikova is a covert FSB agent to spread the narrative of good Russians and the removal of sanctions in the Western press."

My head is spinning. In Russia they accuse me of having ties to the British embassy, and in Ukraine they write that I am an FSB agent. It seems that I have accidentally found myself in the epicenter of the information war. This thought keeps me up all night.

The next morning I go down to the first floor of the hotel. As usual, I agreed to meet Peter for breakfast. We sit alone in the empty hall of a small restaurant.

"Why are you so sad?" Peter asks.

"Rumors started to spread actively in social networks that I am an FSB agent," I say grimly.

"You're not an agent. I knew it right away." Peter laughs.

"That's right. As my son said, I would have blabbed all the secrets," I say, trying for some levity. "What I don't understand is what would be the point of sending an agent to the German newspaper *Welt*? What secrets could they have? What is my role? What can I influence? I have no power, no money!"

"I was just reading what they wrote about you in *Politico*," Peter says with irony in his voice, "*The mysterious case of Marina O. Her anti-war protest was seen by millions on live Russian television. But is she a Kremlin puppet*?"

Peter laughs. He takes his eyes off his smartphone, takes a sip of coffee, and continues reading:

> *In an unremarkable room of a secret police station, a policeman offered Marina Ovsyannikova a cup of tea.*
>
> *"At that moment I wasn't scared," Ovsyannikova told me. "Now I would think twice."*
>
> *Any opponent of President Vladimir Putin, of those who survived, would have warned Ovsyannikova: when a Russian security officer offers you an Earl Grey drink and a snack, don't say yes. But Ovsyannikova was new to the dissident game and was not prepared for what she was about to go through. She drank her tea.*
>
> *Dissident or puppet?*
>
> *The inconsistencies in Marina O's story are staggering: a suddenly awakened conscience forces a veteran propagandist from a central TV station to speak*

out against the regime and ruin her comfortable life. Doubts were raised by the fact that she was given a small fine and allowed to communicate with the Western media.

Of course, one of the consequences of propaganda has been that it is impossible to believe in anything real. The point of Putin's propaganda machine is ambiguity and fear.

Peter looks at me meaningfully and laughs again.

"Make up your mind; what do you prefer? Polonium, Novichok, or just a car crash?" he jokes.

"Stop mocking me. In my situation, you can't take things seriously, or you might just go crazy.

"Why don't we go for a run or look for a gym? As long as we have some free time," I suggest.

An hour later, Peter carefully parks the silver SUV outside a sports club. As he gets out of the car, he tensely looks around.

"Do you think we're being followed?"

"No. I'm just checking, just in case."

"And how can you tell if you're being followed?" I wonder. "I have no such experience. This is the first time I've been caught up in a spy story."

"You'd never guess if you were being professionally tracked. It will be an ordinary family, with children and a dog. The kids will be cranky and ask for ice cream."

"That's funny. I'll keep that in mind."

We walk up the steep stairs to the gym. I go into the spacious locker room, take out my phone, and scroll through my messages. On the screen is a message from my friend Thomas in London: "I began to doubt the sincerity of what you did. It looks like you really are a Kremlin agent. My Ukrainian friends write about it. They don't believe you."

The blood rushes to my face with indignation. Without a second's hesitation, I write back.

"Aren't you ashamed to write me such words? I never thought you could send me such a message. In Moscow I saved your life, and now I have ruined my life for the truth. I am taking a very big risk. Now I'm going to war in Ukraine to help Ukrainians, and you write me this? When the war started, you yourself said, 'Stay on the side of good.' Now I have sacrificed everything for good and freedom."

I send the message. I try to calm down, but I have another attack of nervous coughing.

Trying to cope with the coughing, I go into the cardio area, throw my phone on the windowsill, and start furiously pedaling on the machine.

The phone beeps. There's a new message from Thomas.

"I'm sorry. I didn't mean to offend you. I just wanted to hear it from you. I know you, and I trust you completely."

I don't write anything back. Life is too short to waste it on mutual suspicions and conspiracy theories. All this only plays into the hands of the Kremlin. In the current situation, all opponents of the war, no matter who they are or what they were doing before February 24, must unite and act together.

As I leave the gym, I remember that Christina sent me a scan of her passport.

"Just in case," I tell Peter, "I texted you Christina's passport. I trust her completely; she's taking a big risk by helping me."

The days of waiting are unbearably slow. We've been in Chisinau for a week, but we still can't get into Ukraine.

"My people checked Christina; nothing seems suspicious," Peter tells me at breakfast.

"Great, and I just got the number of a high-ranking Ukrainian official," I say after reading a message from the *Welt.*

"Ask for accreditation as soon as possible," Peter says.

Without a second's hesitation, I write a lengthy message:

"Good afternoon! This is Marina Ovsyannikova. I protested against the war on the air of Channel One. Now I work for the German media concern *Welt.* I really want to help you. I am in Chisinau now and I really want to come to Kiev and do materials about the crimes in Bucha, Irpen, and Borodyanka, maybe go as far as Kharkov. Russians need to know the truth about what is really going on in Ukraine. Maybe I can record an interview with Zelensky. His online interview with Russian journalists, which was recorded in the early days of the war, was incredibly popular. The Russian authorities blocked this interview, but everyone bypassed the blockades and watched it. Zelensky is a hero; he is with his people, not like ours, hiding and sitting in a bunker, afraid to come out to people. I need permission from the Ukrainian government and some kind of escort from the border. Help me, please."

With a sinking heart I send the message and wait for a reply. A few hours later, I get a terse message: "I'm busy right now, but I'll think about it."

The warm spring sun is beating down. Peter is sitting across from me on the open veranda of a small Moldovan restaurant. He monitors all the news coming out of Ukraine nonstop.

"I hope that tomorrow we can finally go to Kiev," I tell him in a hopeful voice.

"Great. Have them give us an escort. Otherwise they'll arrest us at the first checkpoint. Don't forget that you have a Russian passport."

"But it says that I was born in Odesa. My father is Ukrainian."

Peter looks at me like I'm a naïve child.

A few minutes later, a message from *Welt* pops up on my smartphone screen: "They want to give you a media award for freedom. The organizers have contacted us now. They are asking us to record a three-minute video message for the award ceremony."

"In English?" I reply.

"Yes, better in English."

Sitting in my hotel room, I write the text and try to learn it by heart.

"Thank you so much for this award. To be honest, I didn't expect this at all. Let it be awarded for all independent Russian journalists who are fighting against Putin for our freedom..."

I'm trying to record a video. In the background is a white wall and a cheap room closet; it spoils the whole impression. Perhaps this hotel has a small conference room. I go out into the corridor and head in the direction of reception.

There's a man in blue jeans standing by the stairs, staring at me intently. It occurs to me that I did see him before. He was in the first hotel where Peter and I stayed when we arrived in Chisinau. At breakfast, this man was sitting alone, not far from Peter and me. How did he end up here? Was it a coincidence, or was he following us? The thought is unsettling.

When I get downstairs, I send a message about the suspicious stranger to Peter. He rushes out of his room to the front desk, but by this point the man in blue jeans has disappeared.

"You promised you wouldn't go anywhere alone," the security advisor starts chastising me.

After getting coffee, I go up to my room. Peter walks me to the door, just in case. It's drizzling outside, a fine spring rain. The heating in the hotel is off, and I wrap myself in a warm jacket, trying to keep warm.

A call comes in from the *Welt* editorial office. They say, "You know, they decided not to give you the award. We don't understand what's going on at all. That's not the way to do it."

"It's very simple," I explain. "I don't deserve this award. For years I worked for Channel One, the main mouthpiece of Kremlin propaganda. It's a lot easier for people to believe in conspiracy theories than it is to believe in noble gusto. In any case, there are many independent journalists in Russia worthy of this award who have been fighting the Putin regime for years. I am only at the beginning of this journey."

"Is there any news from the Ukrainian official?" they ask on the other end of the line.

"No, almost all of my messages go unanswered. Last time he wrote that he didn't understand why I had to go to Kiev; it seems that all my efforts were in vain. The Russian secret services did everything they could to make sure that no one would believe in the sincerity of my intentions. But I don't want to sit idly by. There are thousands of refugees from Ukraine in Chisinau. Let me do a report for *Welt* from the refugee center and go to the Ukrainian border."

"That's a great idea. In a few days you'll have a film crew flying in from Berlin. And you can start working."

In the morning, together with Peter, we meet two men with a video camera at the hotel reception.

"Let's go to Moldovexpo today," I suggest. "It's the largest exhibition center. They used to house people with Covid there, and now there are more than four hundred refugees from Nikolaev and Odesa living there."

The huge pavilion of the exhibition center is divided by hundreds of partitions made of white cloth. People live in each compartment. Volunteers greet us at the entrance to the pavilion.

"We have mostly women and children here," says an employee of the center. "Some spend the night here and go further to the

EU countries. Others, on the contrary, do not want to go far from home, hoping that soon the shelling will end and they will be able to return."

Together with the videographer, we walk down a long corridor. A group of boys runs past us. An old woman standing by the washing machine looks sternly at them. We go into the children's room. There is a young woman playing with her three-year-old daughter. Everyone looks at us with huge brown eyes full of pain.

"We are from Nikolayev; our dad is at the front, and we miss him very much and want to come home as soon as possible."

A very young girl joins our conversation with her two-year-old son. Her exhausted face is full of anxiety. She tells of fleeing with her child from the suburbs of Odesa. She has not heard from her father or brothers since.

She says, "I want to tell them that I love them very much, and I want to go home very much. As soon as this is all over, we'll definitely come back, sit at the same table with them, and everything will be fine."

Tears roll down her cheeks. She clutches the baby tighter to her. I can hardly keep from bursting into tears, and I leave the playroom. The videographer follows me.

"What did she say?" he asks.

"Sorry. I can't translate." I turn away quickly.

A lump rises up to my throat. I quickly step outside into the darkness. At that moment, I start coughing again.

In the morning we get in the car and drive toward the Ukrainian border. Peter looks intently at the navigator. I am scrolling through the news on my phone. Our colleagues, sitting in the back seat of the car, are discussing something among themselves in German.

On the sides of the road are fields and lonely villages. Moldova is considered the poorest country in Europe. A herd of cows blocks our way. We wait patiently for the animals to cross over to the other side.

"By the way, did you see the explosions in Transnistria?" Peter asks. "It looks like Russia wants to open a second front there."

"Yes, I did. How far is it from here to the Transnistrian border?"

"It's about an hour away. But we can't go there; this enclave is under Russian control."

"I know. You, as a British citizen, will definitely be taken prisoner."

"You'll be arrested there, too."

"Yeah, they'll arrest me in Transnistria, they'll arrest me in Russia, and they won't let me go to Ukraine. Maybe you guys could go to Kiev instead of me?" I jokingly ask my German colleagues.

"No, I'm not going there for any money. I have a family. I have to go back to them," one of them answers quite seriously. "Last month, American journalist Brent Reno died there. You saw yesterday, more Chinese journalists came under fire. The images are chilling."

I turn away and look silently at the road. Around the corner, a field full of white tents appeared.

"Pull over near them," I say to Peter.

At the tent camp we meet a family from Mariupol. Russian troops have practically wiped the city off the face of the earth.

A young man in his thirties takes his wife and daughter aside and returns to us. His gaze makes me feel uncomfortable; his eyes seem to glaze over.

"We were burying our neighbors in flowerbeds, eating pigeons and cats. There was no water, no light, nothing. I was a grown man, crying for the first time in my life. I still can't believe we made it out of that hell. The five of us were traveling in one car, at the exit of the city we were stopped by the Russians. They held us there, forced us to undress completely, and then they let us go. We drove all the way through Ukraine by car. Here at the border, when they found out that we were from Mariupol, they let us out without any questions. They don't let men from eighteen to sixty out of the country, martial law, but they made an exception for us."

The man steps aside; he can't talk anymore. On the way back to Chisinau, we drive in silence. The smell of war is getting stronger and stronger. Finally, I decide to break the silence.

"Guys, you know that all of the refugees we interviewed today answered my questions in proper Russian. Nobody infringed on their rights in Ukraine. They didn't ask Putin to release them. They don't want a 'Russian world.' They want to live in a free and independent country."

"Instead, the 'Russian world' came to them," Peter notes with irony in his voice.

"And liberated them from their apartments and property," I add. "We live in total shit ourselves, and we don't let others live. Have you ever been to Russia? If you go a hundred kilometers away from Moscow, poverty is rampant everywhere. Can you imagine, thirty million Russians live without sewers; they have toilets in the street. In the twenty-first century they use pit latrines. The state can't provide people with basic amenities; people live in wooden barracks. Instead of building normal homes with amenities for its citizens, Russia trashes the homes of Ukrainians."

We park outside the hotel. I'm leaving for Germany tomorrow. Peter is going to Kyiv to guard another reporter. Staying in Chisinau doesn't make sense anymore. I never managed to get accreditation to go to Ukraine.

CHAPTER 15

ABSOLUTE EVIL MUST NOT TAKE OVER THE WORLD

MAY 2022, BERLIN

"In a few minutes our plane will land in Berlin," the flight attendant announces over the speakerphone. I lean against the porthole. There are flat, well-kept fields and small, cozy houses below.

At the enormous Brandenburg Airport, I am met by an employee of the newspaper *Welt*.

"Hi! How was your flight?" He speaks enthusiastically, practically without pauses. "It's this way, this exit. Through our contacts we've arranged for your long-term work visa; we'll have to take a picture and submit the documents...."

Our cab pulls up to a large apartment hotel, and there are two more people waiting for us. We take the elevator up to the fifth floor.

"For security reasons, we put you under a false name. Here's a German SIM card for your phone. You rest for now; we'll talk to you later."

The men leave, and I start unpacking. At that moment, a message pops up on my phone from Jaka Bizilj.

"Hi! Are you already in Berlin?"

"Yes, I just flew in."

"Dinner tonight? Where are you staying? I'll send a cab for you."

"Thank you; that's very kind. My Russian cards don't work because of the sanctions. I can't even use Uber."

I send the address, and a cab arrives half an hour later. The car loops through the streets of Berlin, and I have no idea where I am going. Hours, days, weeks flit by at a cosmic speed. I don't even have a second of free time to study a map of Berlin.

"Nice to meet you." Jaka shakes my hand.

We enter the restaurant. It's lively inside. The waiter struggles to find an empty table for us.

"Have you been to Berlin?"

"No, only to Cologne and Munich. I have traveled through much of Germany in my car. Four years ago we took the whole family on a big road trip across Europe."

I tell Jaka about how I decided to protest live on air and what's going on in Russia right now.

"These people, Putin's supporters, are really zombified by propaganda. They are like sick people who cannot be cured as long as this stream of lies is pouring out of the screen."

"Is it true that Putin can use nuclear weapons?"

"I hope it doesn't come to that. But we are all well aware that the nuclear button is in the hands of a madman."

"A few days ago, Putin warned the West against interfering in the situation in Ukraine and said that retaliatory strikes would be lightning-fast."

"I have heard. The rhetoric of Putin's propagandists particularly scares me. *Russia Today* head Margarita Simonyan threatens the world with World War III. That's exactly what she said on the air yesterday. Can you imagine a woman who is the mother of three children talking about a nuclear strike? Is this possible in a normal civilized society?"

As we talk, our faces darken.

The next day we meet outside the Wall Museum of the East Side Gallery. Jaka built it a few years ago under the inspiration of Mikhail Gorbachev.

"Thirty-two years ago the Berlin Wall collapsed completely unexpectedly; people were fed up with it all," says Jaka.

"Maybe Putin's regime will fall soon, too. If Navalny had been at large, things might have gone differently."

"I told him he didn't have to go back to Russia. He made that decision himself. In general, he is an incredibly brave man."

"You know, the Russian people take a long time to swing. But when the Russian revolt begins, it will be swift and merciless."

After a short tour, we walk along a preserved fragment of the Berlin Wall, admiring the legendary graffiti with Leonid Brezhnev, General Secretary of the Communist Party of the Soviet Union, and Eric Honecker, the leader of the GDR. Then we go to a café on the waterfront and order Bavarian sausages; everything is very simple and democratic.

The next day I go to the *Welt* editorial office for the first time. The young man greeting me speaks Russian with a slight accent: "My mother is Russian. Let's go this way. These are the two buildings of the Axel Springer media company. One is in the East and one is in the West of Berlin. You can see a piece of wall between them."

He shows a wide line running along the sidewalk. We enter one of the glass buildings. At the entrance, my belongings and documents are checked by security.

"Only one guard is posted, not five, like at Ostankino," I remark ironically.

We go up to the fourth floor. There are dozens of computers in the huge newsroom.

"This is the newspaper's editorial office. And upstairs is television. Come on. I'll take you to the dressing room."

A beautiful woman, a makeup artist, comes out to meet us and speaks Russian without an accent.

"And you are from Russia?" I ask; my astonishment is growing.

"Yes, I've lived in Berlin for more than fifteen years."

After recording the interview with the *Welt* staff, we go up to the top floor. There is a noisy buffet in the chamber restaurant. The awards ceremony for young journalists has just ended.

"How did you do that?" asks a very young girl, no more than seventeen years old. "It was incredible. I couldn't believe my eyes."

"And then what happened? Did the guards get you?" asks a guy.

"Will Russia start a nuclear war?"

Questions are pouring in from all directions. I barely have time to answer them, choosing the right English words. It's nearly midnight.

The next day we are making plans for my work with the management of the media group. On May 9, I will have to participate in live broadcasts dedicated to the Victory Parade on Red Square.

"This year's parade will look like a real feast during the plague," I exclaim.

As I return to my hotel room, I think about how difficult it will be for me to talk about this. While Ukrainians sit in basements, Russians with assault rifles will march across the pavement of Red Square. While Ukrainian children tremble at the sound of sirens, Russians smile at the salute. This year's Victory Parade in Moscow will be a triumph of evil.

I'm trying to understand how in these seventy-seven years Russia has turned from a victorious country into an aggressor country. Two of my grandfathers, a Ukrainian and a Russian, fought together on the fronts of the Second World War against fascism. If they were still living and learned that Russia had attacked Ukraine, they would have cursed us, their grandchildren.

On the evening of May 9, I read that Russian troops shelled Odesa again.

"We sat in the basement all evening," I read a message from my cousin in Odesa.

I try to imagine what it would be like to hide from falling shells in a basement with your children. I have nightmares all night long.

I wake up early in the morning and see a message on my phone from Anton Gashinsky, the lawyer: "Good morning! Can you comment on this? Your ex-husband is suing you; the lawsuit is children-related. The first hearing is in six days."

Immediately I dial the lawyer's number.

"Explain to me, what does all this mean? There must be some mistake. It can't be! After the protest, he stopped communicating with me, didn't answer my calls, and blocked me on all messengers. But I thought he did it for safety reasons. That he was just afraid, laying low, but would get in touch later. This is the sneakiness I did not expect from him. He's clearly acting under orders from above. It's a planned attack. I don't believe that the father wants to hurt his children psychologically. Why would the children be involved in this? We are civilized adults; all problems can be solved through negotiations."

"The best way to pressure a woman is with her children," the lawyer replies.

"How low and despicable. He literally stabbed me in the back. I wasn't expecting this turn of events at all. Why did he do it? Why would he do that? Can you tell me why?"

"You're going to have to find another lawyer for family cases. We only do political cases."

"I see." My problems are snowballing.

A few minutes later I call my son. "Hi! What's going on over there?"

"Nothing. It's okay."

"And why did Dad, instead of talking to me, sue me?"

"Really? I didn't know about that. You shouldn't have made a demarche on the air. You're the one who ruined our family's life."

"Putin should not have unleashed a criminal war; then no one would have staged demarches. We have reached the point of no return. All the normal people quit state television after February 24, leaving only the scoundrels. They are the warmongers. And the most important criminal is your father's boss, Margarita Simonyan."

The conversation is clearly not going well. I feel like I'm losing my connection with my son.

"Okay, let's not talk politics. How's the exam preparation going?"

"It's okay." He gives the standard answer.

At this point, I start coughing nonstop, choking up.

"Iz-xx-xx-xx-xx-guilty," I barely squeeze out. "I'll call you back."

The coughing only stops after half an hour. I call my daughter. Her face pops up on the screen.

"Mommy, hi! How are you?"

"I'm okay, my little sunshine."

"When are you coming back?"

"Soon, I promise you, in two weeks, a month at the most. It depends on my work."

"But it's been two weeks now."

"I know, my beauty. It's just that circumstances are such that I can't go back yet. Most likely, school will end now, and you will come to me for the vacations. We'll go to Italy or Spain."

"My dad will never let me go. He doesn't want to get me a new passport."

"Why?"

"He says it's dangerous in Europe. Russians are hated there, attacked."

"That's not true; you know that. No one is attacking the Russians. These rumors are purposely spread by *Russia Today*, where your daddy works, and other Kremlin channels, so that the Russians will rally around Putin and think that all around them are enemies. Don't believe it, my sweetie; no one here will hurt you. You and I have been to Europe many times."

"Yes, I remember how you lost me at the Eiffel Tower," jokes Arisha, remembering our family trips to Europe.

I do not respond to her jokes. At this point I am absolutely certain that my ex-husband, who works in the top management of the propaganda monster *Russia Today*, has turned his children into a tool of pressure. My son is about to turn eighteen and will be able to fly to me on his own. But my little girl is only eleven. And I have to find a way to meet her. It's impossible to take her anywhere without a passport. It's a dead end. It looks like I won't be able to see my daughter until the Putin regime collapses.

All day long I am depressed and unable to concentrate on my work. It is only in the evening that I remember that I had promised CNN to comment on the actions of Lenta.ru state media staffers Yegor Polyakov and Alexandra Miroshnikova. On May 9, they told the Russians the truth by publishing anti-war articles. The website's home page with the headlines "Putin Unleashed One of the Bloodiest Wars of the 21st Century" and "Vladimir Putin Turned into a Pathetic Dictator and Paranoid" was deleted immediately. The journalists fled Russia.

Pulling myself together, I appear on CNN in the evening. After the interview, I pull on my tracksuit and go for a run. On the promenade I involuntarily look around to see if I am being followed. I need to run at least seven kilometers today. Because of the constant stress I am rapidly losing my fitness.

On the way back I notice a man of Slavic appearance in the hotel lobby. This morning I saw him outside the entrance to the *Welt* Media Group building. A chill runs down my spine.

I tell Jaka Bizilj about the suspicious stranger.

"Report it to the police," he advises.

"Why? I don't have time. I need to finish a special report on propaganda methods on Russian television. I've arranged an interview with my former colleague Zhanna Agalakova. After that I will fly to Oslo for the Václav Havel Award for Creative Protest. And then straight to Odesa."

I take the elevator up to my room and contact Agalakova via Skype. On February 24, she published a post on social media, saying, "This war is not in my name." Management demanded its removal. Zhanna, who worked as Channel One's own correspondent in France, immediately quit. On my laptop screen she appears in a spectacular red jacket.

"Tell me, when you worked in New York, what was it that made you most angry? I remember that your work lately was mostly limited to covering UN Security Council meetings," I ask her.

"Even before 2014, before the start of the war in Donbass, it became clear that no good, positive news from America was expected from me. President Obama's second term was approaching, and relations between our countries were rapidly deteriorating. When Crimea was annexed, it became even more difficult. My job really came down to covering the UN Security Council meetings. Points of view other than pro-Russian were kept to a minimum. You couldn't be the first to quote an American representative in a report, for example. Or the British one. Or any other whose position was different from the official Russian one. Only the Russian ambassador could be the first to speak from the conference room. And he must have the last word. And all the quotes of the opponents were 'convenient' for his counter-attack. If the statement of the Russian envoy was not very convincing, or if the vote was not in our favor, the editors said, 'Well, the Security Council session is not the reason for the reportage.' And the topic was swept under the carpet. All this, of course, was at odds with what I had been taught in journalism school, how a journalist should work in general."

Next, on the screen of my laptop appears the famous political scientist Abbas Gallyamov. He is outside of Russia, so he can speak freely without fear of persecution.

"In my opinion, the groups of opponents and supporters of the war in Russia are about the same. There are many more people who are undecided, the so-called hesitant majority. It is for their opinion there is a real struggle," the political scientist explains. "Technically speaking, yesterday the entire First Channel was patriotic, and now it turns out that the employees of Channel One turn out to be absolute oppositionists in their rear. And this kind of thing creates a sense of momentum. It means that the oppositionists are no longer marginalized; they have already infiltrated there. You know, this is what's called 'the spirit of the era,' and if you manage to articulate a sense that the spirit of the era is opposition, then that will actually be a victory."

I slam the lid on my laptop and start packing. The information war for the hearts and minds of Russians is in full swing. The ultimate evil must not be allowed to take over the world. At this point I decide that I am going to be as detailed as possible about how propaganda is spread on Russian television. The more people in Russia know how their minds are manipulated, the less they will believe the lies that are broadcast at the behest of the Kremlin.

"Polonium or Novichok?" I remembered the guard's words. "Or will it be a car crash? Or maybe an accident? This man will just come up to the room and throw me off the balcony...." The thought rattles around in my head.

CHAPTER 16

FREEDOM FORUM

MAY 24–27, 2022

"Welcome to the Freedom Forum in Norway," a pretty American woman greets me. "I will be your chaperone. How nice that you were able to come after all."

Our car pulls away from Oslo Airport and glides smoothly down the perfectly smooth road. Fields and trees with sparse northern vegetation flash by outside the window. I look at the unfamiliar landscapes with interest and remember that Norway is one of the most prosperous countries in Europe, the most socially oriented state. In Norway, there is no such strong stratification of society into rich and poor as in Russia.

"I just flew in yesterday from New York." My attendant smiles broadly.

"That's great. I've never been to New York. More than twenty years ago I studied in the United States, just for two months. It was an internship in efficient television production in California, Washington, and Oregon. I remember being shocked when we arrived at some regional TV studio that was many times better equipped than the Russian federal channels. Technologically, we were way behind at the time. And now, because of the war and sanctions, Russia is sliding into the abyss."

Our car pulls up to a posh hotel in downtown Oslo. In the lobby, a musician in a black tuxedo plays the piano. On the right-hand side of the restaurant, I can see gentlemen in fine suits and elegant ladies.

"You're scheduled to present during dinner tonight." The chaperone checks the schedule. "And tomorrow night is the awards ceremony."

"I have to prepare my speech in English," I say. "It's such a huge stage. I might get confused. I have no experience speaking at such events."

"Don't worry; we'll have a rehearsal. Send me the slides of your presentation. I'll help you."

In my hotel room, I write my speech for the awards ceremony, looking for the right slides online. Everything happening at this moment seems completely unreal to me.

The organizers of the Freedom Forum and I are backstage. There are bottles of water, coffee, and sandwiches on the table. I am introduced to the other recipients of the Vaclav Havel Prize for Creative Protest—Turkish-American basketball player Enes Kanter Freedom and the creators of the PaykanArtCar project, who advocate for human rights in Iran.

On the side there are three giant statuettes—scaled-down copies of the Statue of Liberty in New York. One of the forum organizers, smiling, picks up a statue and warns us: "Grab it with both hands; it's heavy."

"Wow, I think it's twenty kilograms." I can barely hold it in my hands.

"You all will have to order extra luggage," jokes the organizer.

The people standing around us are laughing.

At that moment they call me to the stage. I step out into a huge space flooded with footlights. Hundreds of eyes are looking at me. My voice trembles with excitement.

> Thank you so much for this award!
>
> When I first read George Orwell's novel *1984*, I was a journalism student.
>
> This is a social fiction. In future Russia, that would be impossible, I thought. It was 1998, at the time of Yeltsin's democratic reforms. Now it seems like ages ago.
>
> I really was wrong! In just twenty years, Russia has turned into a totalitarian state. Now people are being jailed for saying, "No war!" And the president of this country is a real war criminal.
>
> In twenty years, Putin has destroyed all independent media in Russia. Instead, he built a cynical and lying propaganda machine. It works in accordance with Goebbel's philosophy of constantly calling black white. Propaganda media dehumanizes people. For years, pro-government media have instilled in Russians hatred toward the people of Ukraine, the United States, and Western Europe. We all know what a great disaster this led to.
>
> February 24 was the point of no return for me. It was a shock.
>
> After my live broadcast protest, my children said that I had ruined our family's life. And they kept asking me why I did it.
>
> In this life one must sometimes do the seemingly irrational for the greater good.

> I want my children to live in a free country that does not attack neighbors in the dead of night and does not threaten the whole world with nuclear weapons.
>
> I know what millions of Ukrainian women and children are experiencing right now.
>
> I know what it's like to lose everything and become a refugee. I experienced the same thing when I was a teenager as the first war in Chechnya began. My house was reduced to rubble.
>
> That's why I hate war. Any war is death, pain, and ruined lives.
>
> Orwell wrote the fastest way to end a war is to lose it. It's hard for me to talk about it, but I want my country to lose the war as soon as possible. I don't see any other way.
>
> The light must triumph over darkness.
>
> Thanks again for this award. I wish to use this money to help Ukrainian refugees.

In two months, the organizers of the forum will transfer my part of the $12,000 prize to the volunteer fund in Moldova, which organized the transportation of refugees from Odesa and Nikolaev to the European Union.

"Come to dinner tonight," the organizers invite me.

There is music playing in the restaurant, and dozens of dissidents from all over the world have gathered under one roof. The spirit of absolute freedom reigns here.

"Hi, I am a dissident from Cuba. Can I take selfies with you?"

"Hi, I'm a reporter for the *Washington Post*. I'd like to record an interview with you."

A man hands me his business card. In the maelstrom of numerous acquaintances, I try to remember new faces and names.

"Hi, I'm an assistant...," a short young man says the name of a famous Russian oligarch. "It is a pleasure to meet you. And this is my friend; he is Ukrainian. He lives in New York."

"How interesting. I just now want to go to Ukraine as a journalist."

"We can help you. We're working with American human rights activists who are now in Kiev."

"Great. I happened to meet one of the creators of the NTV channel on social media. After Putin came to power, Savely¶ emigrated to London and now lives in Odesa. His wife is Ukrainian. So he promised to help me with filming in Odesa. I'm flying to my hometown after Oslo. I will meet him there. And then I don't know how to get to Kiev."

"We'll put you in touch with the right people," say my new acquaintances as we say goodbye.

¶ Name changed

CHAPTER 17

THE PRESS CONFERENCE THAT NEVER HAPPENED

MAY 28–JUNE 2, 2022, UKRAINE

At the passport control in Chisinau, there is a familiar border guard. When he recognizes me, he smiles broadly and lets me through without asking too many questions.

In the arrivals hall, a short-haired redheaded man comes up to me.

"Hi, I'm Nick**." He introduces himself as the security advisor. We're going to be working together.

Nick rushes off toward the parking lot. Without any hesitation, I follow him.

The hands of the clock are approaching midnight. Through the dark streets of Chisinau we drive to the booked hotel.

"Are you also from Great Britain?" I ask.

"Yes, but I live in Portugal now."

"And you guard journalists because you have combat experience."

** Name changed

"Yes, I served in Iraq. How did you know that?"

"Don't be frightened; your colleague told me everything while we were stuck in Chisinau."

Nick laughs out loud.

"Tomorrow morning at 10:00 a.m.," I tell him, "they'll be waiting for us at the Palanka border checkpoint, and we'll go to Odesa."

"Then we leave at 8:00 a.m.," he says. "It takes us about two hours to get to the border."

In the morning, our car pulls up to the checkpoint. In front of us are several cars with Ukrainian license plates. In spite of the constant shelling, these are people who have decided to return home. A man in uniform is walking leisurely alongside the cars. As we approach, he takes our documents and asks to open the trunk. When he sees two huge cans of gasoline, the border guard gets indignant.

"We are not allowed to carry more than twenty liters of gasoline."

"But there's no fuel in Ukraine," Nick tries to argue. "We can't fill up anywhere."

"I don't care about that. We have rules," the border guard says.

Nick has no choice but to leave the gas cans at customs. After that they let us through.

"And I recognize you," the Ukrainian border guard says, smiling. "Were you the one who was on Russian television with the poster?"

"Yes." I nod. "Now, as a journalist, I'm going to my native Odesa."

"Can I take a picture with you?" he asks.

We step aside and take selfies. The border guard gives us our passports and wishes us a safe journey.

A police escort car is waiting for us on the Ukrainian side. Without stopping past numerous checkpoints with anti-tank hedgehogs, we race toward Odesa. We glimpse houses with sandbags on their windows along the side of the road.

A phone call comes in. It's Savely.

"I am waiting for you. Have you crossed the border yet?"

"Yes, just now."

"Download a special app on your phone that alerts you to air alerts. I'll send you the link right now."

I download the app. My phone starts howling nonstop; red signals pop up on the screen:

Alert. Kyiv region. All in shelters
Alert. Cherkassy region. All in shelters
Alert. Mykolaiv region. All in shelters
Alert. Odesa region. All in shelters

I call Savely from another phone.

"How can I stop it? The sirens are howling nonstop."

"You select only Odesa in the settings; delete the rest," he advises. "Come straight to my house. I'll meet you. Your hotel is right next to my house, right on the waterfront."

Our car winds through the streets of Odesa. I look out the window and remember the last time I was in this beautiful seaside city twenty years ago.

Then our huge liner sailed along the Crimean coast and moored in the port of Odesa. On board were filmmakers from Russia, Ukraine, and other CIS countries. They were all taking part in an international film festival. At that time I was still a young reporter from Krasnodar, and our film crew was covering the film festival. Together with famous actors and directors we walked around Deribasovskaya Street and enjoyed the local color. None of us could have imagined that in just twelve years Putin would tear the Crimean peninsula from Ukraine and destabilize Donbass. And in another eight years he would start a full-scale war.

Our car pulls up to a new apartment building. Savely meets us near the supermarket.

"Hey, how was your trip? Come on. I'll show you to your hotel."

"It's so crazy! I was looking at that app you told me to download the whole way. They are bombarding the entire territory of Ukraine without stopping, and they brazenly lie to us. Putin is just cynically destroying Ukrainians. This is real genocide!"

"Lavrov (the Russian foreign minister) recently confessed," Savely says, "that they want to take over the entire south of Ukraine, the Kherson, Mykolaiv, and Odesa regions, and go to the unrecognized Transnistria. But we will not give them Odesa! Let them not even hope...."

The three of us, Savely, Nick, and I, go down to the sea and walk along the promenade. Everything seems to be normal. Children are laughing, a few teenagers pass us on electric scooters, and a guy and a girl in tracksuits run toward us. Only near the shoreline hang red signs: "Beware of mines."

"They are bombarding us from the sea, over there. Rockets fly low over the sea. After the Ukrainian Armed Forces hit the Moskva cruiser, the Russian warships moved away from the shore, afraid. They used to be visible right from the windows of my apartment. Here's your hotel; make yourself comfortable. If you want, you can sunbathe by the pool."

Savely points to the side. By the small pool a few vacationers are lying on white plastic lounge chairs, enjoying the warm rays of the May sun.

"Aren't they scared?" I am amazed.

"There is an air defense system working over the city. At first we were hiding in basements, but now we're used to it. No one hides anymore during air raid alarms."

"Why?"

"Everyone was tired and, you could say, used to it. The town was deserted in the first days of the war, and now people have started to return home. My neighbors say the risk of being killed in an air strike is about the same as dying in a car crash."

"No, I don't agree with you; the risk is much higher."

We agree with Savely that tomorrow he will show us around the city.

Late at night we meet a cameraman from Kiev in the parking lot outside the hotel. A thin man of medium height gets out of a small gray Ford covered with a thick layer of dust.

"Sergey," he introduces himself. "Actually, I was waiting for you in Kiev. But I got a message from Berlin that I had to go to Odesa urgently."

"Yes, we'll work here for a couple of days. And then they'll send an escort car for us and we'll go to Kiev," I clarify.

At six o'clock in the morning, the air-raid siren wails frantically on the phone. I jump out of bed, open the curtain, and look out the window. On the horizon, gloomy clouds merge with the blackness of the sea. There is an ominous silence.

The phone rings. It's Savely.

"Are you awake yet? A missile attack is possible. They write that several warships have moved from the Crimea toward Odesa." His voice sounds troubled.

"Are you scaring me on purpose? What should we do? Where do we run to? Where do we hide? In the hotel basement?"

"I don't think there's any point in running. If it comes, you'll be trapped in the basement and you won't be able to get out."

"I think so too, but I don't want to die."

"Everything will be fine," Savely encourages me. "We'll meet at 10:00 at the reception, as agreed. I'll take you to the Russian consulate first."

The four of us approach the car. Savely explains to the British security guard our route, laid out in the navigator. The cameraman puts his tripod in the trunk, and I look at the map of the shelling on my phone. Almost the entire territory of Ukraine is marked in red.

The car loops through the streets of Odesa. At one of the intersections I notice a large billboard. "Russian Soldier Stop! Don't kill lives for Putin. Go home with a clear conscience." I take a photo and post it on my social networks.

A few minutes later, Nick parks our SUV near a red brick fence. "Irpen, Bucha, Mariupol," it says on the wall in giant black letters.

"From the windows of my apartment I saw Russian diplomats burning documents two days before the war began, and then fleeing from here," Savely tells us.

The doors of the Russian consulate are tightly closed. There are soldiers of the military defense on duty near the entrance.

"Let's go and show you the ruined hotel," Savely suggests. "A Russian shell landed there last month. It's a good thing no one was there at the time."

We drive to the outskirts of town. Right on the very shore stands a long two-story building. The middle section of the hotel is completely destroyed.

"It looks like they wanted to destroy the communication tower, which stands on the mountain, and ended up here," remarks our Ukrainian colleague, getting out of the car.

The wind sways the sign that reads "Mines." It hangs on a thin iron chain that blocks the entrance to the hotel grounds.

There is not a living soul around us. The beach is completely empty. Only a pack of hungry dogs strolls along the road in the distance, watching us intently. Sergey aims his camcorder at them. The dogs freeze for a second, and then, with their tails between their legs, they run away and begin to howl. I get scared.

"Let's go back to town," I suggest to my companions.

We get in the car again and drive toward the ruined apartment building. Before Easter an entire family died there. The father of the family had gone out to get bread, and when he came back, there was a black hole where their apartment had been. His wife, three-month-old daughter, and grandmother were dead.

When we drive up to the apartment building, we hear the sound of a grinder. Only one section of the house was damaged, so the builders are hurriedly restoring the collapsed ceilings. A young woman with a stroller comes out of the entranceway.

"Of course, I'm afraid, but I have nowhere to go," she says. "Our apartment is in another entranceway, it survived, but at the moment of the impact all the walls trembled and plaster fell from the ceiling. All the relatives started calling me, asking how we were. The baby Kira died; she was the same age as my daughter and we used to go for walks together."

The woman leans into the stroller and adjusts the pink blanket. Her daughter looks curiously at Sergey and his small video camera.

I start coughing nervously again. I put my head down, step aside, and notice several burnt-out cars.

"Are you all right?" Nick asks.

"Yes. I've arranged for people from Kiev to come tomorrow morning to pick us up."

"There's something I have to show you before we leave, so let's go to the car."

Nick opens the trunk, stuffed to the brim with canisters, helmets, body armor, and tents, and pulls out a huge bag of medical supplies.

"Here is a tourniquet to stop the bleeding. Painkilling injections..." he begins to explain.

"Why are you showing me this?" I interrupt him. "I don't have a medical degree. I'm a journalist. Do you know how to use it yourself?"

"Of course," replies Nick.

"That's good. Then you'll save me!"

The next morning, two men and a woman are waiting for me at the hotel reception.

"I recognized you," says a woman with long, curly hair, wearing a gray-green jacket. "My name is Lisa[††] and I am a volunteer from the Netherlands. I help refugees. I have my own charitable foundation. And this is Yaroslav[‡‡]. He is Ukrainian and he works with American human rights activists."

"It's nice to meet you," I say.

"Let's have you ride with us in the car, and your bodyguard can follow us," says Yaroslav.

"He's not a bodyguard; he's a security advisor," I clarify.

"Okay," Yaroslav says. "Nick, keep up with us; stay as close to our car as possible. We will pass the roadblocks without stopping; we have a special secret code."

We get into a black Mercedes. The driver pulled off and into the road, and we raced down the highway toward Kiev, maneuvering through the stream of cars.

"It's the trendiest color of the season," I joke as I put on my khaki jacket. "Zelensky prefers only this color. I bought it in

†† Name changed
‡‡ Name changed

Chisinau when I was going to go to Ukraine for the first time. But then I didn't get to do it."

"In general, you're a hero," says Yaroslav. "You sacrificed everything in order to tell the truth."

"Yes, I was left without a home and without a steady job. My ex-husband sued me and wants to take my children away from me. I think he is acting under orders from above."

"Protesting live on air is an act of incredible courage. How did you decide to do that?" Lisa asks.

Once again I, jokingly, give all the details of the protest. All the way through, we laugh. It's a kind of protective mental reaction that helps us not to lose our minds from all the horror going on around us. Our car easily passes small checkpoints one by one. At the big ones, the driver slows down a bit and whispers a secret word to the men in camouflage.

"Do you want to talk to Ukrainian journalists?" Lisa asks me.

"Of course. I have absolutely nothing to hide."

"Maybe we could organize a little press conference, invite a few journalists?" she asks.

"Go ahead. I'd love to."

"Then I will organize everything on the basis of Interfax and write a press release."

"Are you sure that is a good idea?" I ask cautiously. "Interfax is a Russian agency, and they will report it to Moscow. There will be a scandal."

"They are not subordinate to Moscow."

"In general, I plan to work in Ukraine as a *Welt* journalist. I want to go to Bucha, Irpen, maybe even to Kharkov."

"It's very dangerous in Kharkov."

"I know; help me. A family lives there—Karina with her husband and ten-year-old son. Their apartment was bombed and they don't have any belongings. She wrote to me on Instagram, asking for help to get out to Europe. I found them a place in France and sent her money so they could get their passports made."

"Don't worry; of course we will help them. I have a way to get refugees out of Kharkov."

Our car pulls into the underground parking lot of the hotel in the center of Kiev. We take the elevator with our suitcases up to the first floor.

"I'm Amber[§§]," a young, blond American woman introduces herself. "I'm very glad you've joined us. Our people will protect you."

In the lobby of a luxurious five-star hotel in the distance are several bearded, tall men in camouflage with machine guns.

"Then we'll announce the press conference tomorrow," says Lisa. "It's too late today."

We take the elevator with Nick up to the fifth floor.

"I'm going into town to look for petrol," Nick says. Back at the hotel, he shows me a video of a kilometer-long line outside a petrol station in Kiev.

In the morning, a message arrives from Lisa: "We gave the announcement of the press conference. And something unbelievable started to happen. Interfax got a call from Moscow and started making threats. The girl who takes requests is also threatened. She says that she has never encountered anything like this before. Threats come both from Moscow and from Ukrainian journalists. They call you a propagandist and an FSB agent. We had to cancel the press conference because of the negative public response."

I open social networks and start reading. A wave of hatred with constant insults to me poured out in a continuous stream.

---

§§ Name changed

"Ovsyannikova is involved in the Kremlin's manipulation and psychological operations. She calls for the removal of sanctions."

"The Union of Journalists of Ukraine calls for stripping Ovsyannykova of the Václav Havel Prize."

"Where is the Security Service? We need to arrest the propagandist immediately and interrogate her."

I walked quickly around the small room, blood pulsing in my temples. I take a sedative out of my bag. A call from an unfamiliar Moscow number pops up on my messenger.

"Hello, Marina Vladimirovna. These are journalists from Kommersant. We want to invite you to the conference. It will be held online."

"Conference on what topic?"

"About Russophobia."

"I have something to say about this. There is no Russophobia in Europe; this topic is deliberately inflated by the propaganda media so that Russians will rally around Putin."

"I need your prior consent; a person from our editorial office will contact you later. You can confirm your consent then."

The person on the other end of the line is stretching the words and clearly stalling for time. I hang up and think for a second.

What the hell is Kommersant? My name is banned in Russia. Who called me? What was that strange phone call?

Without wasting a second, I knock on the next room and tell Nick about it. He looks at me, surprised. "Don't you know that with the help of special equipment you can calculate a person's whereabouts in just a few minutes? Why are you answering numbers you don't know?"

"I can sometimes be too trusting," I answer, realizing that I had done something stupid.

"I don't know, more likely the FSB was trying to figure out where you were."

A chill runs down my spine. Nick walks around the room like an enraged tiger. "We have to leave right away at five a.m. tomorrow," he says. "I know guys from the SBU called; there are too many threats on social networks. The situation is becoming very dangerous. They will escort us to the border with Poland."

"Why Poland and not back to Moldova?" I whine. "I left some of my things in the Chisinau hotel. I left a heavy statuette in my backpack, which I was given at the Freedom Forum."

"What's more important to you, some fucking statue or your own life?" Nick asks.

"All right, forget the statue. We'll go wherever you say."

We go down to the first floor. The bearded men with machine guns are no longer in the lobby. There is an oppressive silence.

"Where have our guards disappeared to?" I ask Nick in a worried voice, looking around.

"I don't know. Damn it," he curses. "They were here two hours ago."

"It's very strange. Neither Lisa nor Yaroslav are answering me. What's going on?"

We go into a café and sit down at a table. At that moment a text message arrives from an unknown number: "The adviser to the Minister of the Interior wants to meet with you."

"I'm sorry, but I don't want to meet with representatives of law enforcement agencies. I wanted to meet with journalists," I write back, frightened by everything that was going on.

After a while, a message appears on the newswires: "Marina Ovsyannikova is included in the 'Peacemaker' database of enemies of Ukraine. She participates in information and psychological operations of the Kremlin."

"Nick, this is an information war. Nobody believes me. Tell me which prison I should go to, the Russian one or the Ukrainian one?"

"Why Ukrainian? You want to help them, don't you? I don't understand anything," the Briton asks, surprised.

"In social networks they write that I should be put in jail because I was engaged in propaganda."

"The world has gone crazy. We leave tomorrow at 5:00 sharp. The guys from the SBU refused to accompany us."

"Why? What happened?"

"They don't want to take any chances."

"Are we going alone?"

"There is no other way out. We have to leave as soon as possible."

"Then let's go to Chisinau, if we're going alone."

"Good," Nick replies dryly, straining to read another message from his boss.

In the evening, I pull back the heavy curtains and go out on the balcony. The darkness of night slowly descends on the city. The roads are deserted. A curfew has begun in Kiev.

I fall into a shallow sleep for a couple of hours. One by one I have nightmares. I wake up at three in the morning, turn on the bedside lamp, and start reading the news.

"They shelled Liman, Nikolaev, Chernigov, and Odesa regions..."

At 4:45 a.m., the air-raid siren sounds on the phone: *Alert – Kiev – All in bomb shelters*.

My heart is pounding. I jump out into the corridor, knocking on the next room.

"Nick, we have to run. Why don't we hide in the underground parking lot?"

Nick silently grabs a huge khaki bag and runs out the door. We take the elevator downstairs. The air-raid sirens go silent.

Nick throws things into the car, and we head off into the unknown.

"We can't go through nine checkpoints. We'll get shot at or arrested," I whine, hiding in the back of the car.

"I'm going to talk some sense into them. I am a British journalist. I have accreditation, and you are my interpreter. The most important thing is that they don't realize you have a Russian passport. Pretend that you are sound asleep."

Trees flashed along the edges of the road. The first roadblock loomed up ahead. Nick pulled up beside a tall, thick man in camouflage.

"Hi! How are you?" Nick smiles at him like an old friend. "My name is Nick. We were working on the front line. It was dangerous."

Nick holds out his accreditation card to the checking soldier. At that moment, he notices me. I lie on the suitcase with my eyes closed and pretend to be asleep.

"Show me your passports," the checker asks.

Nick, continuing to smile and chat nonstop, holds out his blue British passport to him.

"And your passport?" The soldier looks at me sternly.

I slowly open my eyes, take my black-covered Russian passport out of my bag and quickly unfold it on the page with the German humanitarian visa. The checker looks at the visa, then turns his gaze to me.

I smile and chat casually with Nick.

The soldier takes another hard look at us and leisurely hands our passports back.

"Goodbye, buddy," Nick shouts to him and sharply presses the gas pedal.

The SUV leaves behind a cloud of dust.

"Yay, it worked," I shout with joy. "He didn't realize I had a Russian passport. I think he thought I was English. It's only eight checkpoints to the border. Maybe we'll get lucky."

"Of course we will," Nick shouts back. "Everything will be fine; we'll get through it."

At each checkpoint, my companion put on an act. He told the men colorfully about his service in Iraq, asking where to get gasoline and how to find the nearest store. The inspectors listened intently to our English, got a little embarrassed, and tried to tell us the way in broken English. No one asked me for my passport anymore.

"Nick, you should get an Oscar," I applaud loudly as we safely pass the last checkpoint. "You really saved my life. It's only a matter of time before we cross the border. Just in case, I texted my lawyer and asked for his help. How long do you think the interrogation will last? In Moscow they interrogated me for fourteen hours."

"Wow! I hope they let you go faster in Ukraine."

Ahead of us appears the familiar Palanka border checkpoint. Our car has its nose at the end of a small line. The June sun beats down. Nick opens the windows and shuts off the engine. We wait.

The young border guard takes me to a small office.

"Let me see your phones," he says.

"Please." I enter the passwords into both phones and give them to him. "I have nothing to hide."

The guy studies the contents of the messages with interest. It seems that he has never seen so many contacts from different countries in his life.

"Don't be surprised. After my protest, complete strangers, mostly journalists, write to me. We have a common enemy, and he sits in the Kremlin. We have all become hostages of Putin, who has gone mad and is threatening the world with nuclear weapons. You defend your homeland. In Ukraine there are lines lined up at military recruitment centers, and in Russia, there are burning military recruitment centers; no one wants to die for Putin."

After a two-hour conversation, the border guard reports upstairs that everything is in order. We take selfies to say goodbye; he gives us our documents and lets us go.

Getting in the car, I start reading the news.

"Can you imagine," I say to Nick, "officials in Ukraine suggest that I should be banned from entering the country. And in Russia, the speaker of the State Duma said that I should be deprived of my citizenship. These are my personal results of the fight against this senseless war."

My security guard shrugs his shoulders.

Late at night we arrive at the hotel in Chisinau. Nick is on the phone discussing possible ways to evacuate me to Germany.

I go into the hotel room, incredibly tired, and start to unpack my suitcase. At that moment there is a knock on the door. Nick runs in and yells, "It's urgent; we're leaving."

"What happened? Where to?"

"Romania. Don't ask unnecessary questions."

I quickly shove my things back into the suitcase, and Nick grabs it and runs down the stairs. I can barely keep up with him, so I run after him, stuffing the rest of my things into the bag. A can of hairspray falls out and rolls noisily down the stairs. The cleaning lady sees us off with a surprised look.

Jumping into the car, I yell, "What the hell is going on? Why the rush?"

"It's dangerous here; our security service decided to send you to Germany as soon as possible. Your plane leaves the Romanian airport in two hours; your ticket is already bought. I'll accompany you, but I'm going to Poland. I have to return the car."

Like mad, we rush to the airport and get stuck at the Moldovan-Romanian border.

"Let us through, please," I plead with the border guards. "We're late for our flight."

The border guards give us an indifferent look. No one is in a hurry except us.

"You shouldn't have asked them; now they're going to be checking on us for a long time on purpose," Nick grumbles.

Twenty minutes later, we get our documents back. By some miracle, at the last minute I catch the flight to Berlin.

CHAPTER 18

BULLYING

JUNE 2022, BERLIN

"When can I edit the stories from Odesa? I already have the text ready. I need an editor," I write to my colleagues as soon as my plane lands in Berlin.

My message remains unanswered.

It's Friday. I haven't slept in two days and I'm exhausted, but work is work.

At the hotel, I put the phone close to my pillow and lie on the bed without undressing, waiting for an answer. I'm ready to rush to the newsroom any minute. I open my eyes on Saturday morning. No answer. The day passes in silence. The phone stays silent on Sunday, too. I don't know what to think. Finally, on Monday evening a message comes: "*Welt* management is expecting you at 4:00 p.m. tomorrow."

There's no word about the editing and my material from Odesa. This is all very strange. In anticipation of the appointment, I flip through my newsfeed and social media. But the more I dive into the comments under my posts or posts where my name appears, the scarier it gets. The comments are spewing venom;

their authors are not shy in their expressions. And most stunning of all, this harassment has united Russians and Ukrainians. They have turned against me with equal fury. Some of them are saying that I am being paid by the West; others are saying that I am an FSB agent, and still others are saying that I am a propagandist who never turns out to be former. In short, I am an enemy to all.

I instinctively shrink into a ball, desperately searching for one positive comment. I want to close my eyes, wake up, disappear, or just die. I just physically feel a huge, scary wave coming over me, and I am unable to breathe.

Why? Please stop! Why?

I go to the meeting with *Welt*'s management, completely exhausted. There are two people sitting at a long table. Their faces are focused. I still hope that we will talk about the material shot in Ukraine.

"You know," begins one of them in a soft voice, "we thought we could keep you safe. We're too small a publication; you need to find a bigger employer."

"Maybe you'll get on with writing the book, like you planned? We'll support you financially for another three months, as we agreed."

A lump comes to my throat. I realize I'm all alone. Completely, utterly alone. I lower my eyes and silently walk out of the office.

Already downstairs, on my way out of the newsroom, I bump into a familiar journalist. He looks at me, frightened. I probably don't look good right now.

"I just got fired," I say. "I came back from Ukraine, and nobody wanted my material. Tell me, what was going on while I was away?"

"Ukrainians were protesting again. There was a flurry of negative comments on the *Welt* website and on social networks. They are demanding that you be fired. They even created a petition against you on Change.org. We've never had anything like this."

"Then everything is clear. The Kremlin destroyed its enemy with the hands of its enemies." I say goodbye and walk sullenly toward my hotel. A message from an unknown Ukrainian number pops up on my smartphone screen: "Good afternoon, I am Olesya Medvedeva from strana.ua. I would like to record an interview with you for our publication."

I feel like this is a chance. Finally I can explain everything, I think, a little more cheerful. I'm not an enemy of Ukraine; this is a mistake, a misunderstanding. I will tell them everything, and they will realize that they are victims of the Kremlin's dirty manipulations.

We arrange the interview by Skype.

Half an hour later, there is a call. On my laptop screen is a dark window.

"I can't see you," I say.

"I don't need video. I will only record audio," replies a pleasant female voice. "We are an online print publication."

Within an hour, I answer all questions frankly. Several days go by. The interview does not come out. I write a message to the Ukrainian number.

"Olesya, when is the interview coming out?"

Message not delivered. The number is blocked.

It is when I realize that it was a sitting duck.

I feel something is wrong and start searching for this interview online. By chance I find a video on YouTube. All the questions are vocalized, and my answers are taken out of context. In the subtitles they call me a propagandist, and under the video there are dozens of negative comments in Ukrainian.

In utter despair, I lock myself in my hotel room, hide from everyone, and try not to go outside. The nervous coughing fits start in the early morning and don't stop until late at night. I need help from a doctor, but I have given up on myself. I spend all day on the internet, feverishly scrolling through the news feed.

"The fate of those who left Russia for the 'free world' is unenviable," propagandist Dmitry Kiselev broadcasts on the TV channel Russia. "They are persecuted as Russians, forced to repent all the time, abandoning their homeland, and no one is satisfied. This is the same Marina Ovsyannikova, who jumped out with a cardboard poster into the studio of the live broadcast of the program 'Vremya.' In Russia she was fined by the court, but in the West, she was instantly recognized as a hero. Apparently, having mixed up something, Ovsyannikova left her children, flattered by Europe.

"In Germany, she first got a job at *Welt*, but then demonstrations of idle Ukrainians demanded that she be fired. In short, she didn't work out at *Welt*. She went to Ukraine. It was even worse there. The website 'Peacemaker' put Ovsyannikova in its database, which is a bad sign in terms of security. And there's real bullying online....

"From Kiev, Ovsyannikova rushed to Odesa. There, a press conference and also organized hostility against her. So the trace of Ovsyannikova began to get lost. From the latest that became known. They write that the blond is proposed to bring to the octagon, a ring for fighters of mixed martial arts, plates with the names of fighters. This is done in an open leotard. Somewhere in America, I think. Maybe it's a joke. One way or another, but the results of the casting have not yet been reported," Kiselev reports with a sneer in his voice.

I feel like I am losing my mind. In an effort to protect me, Christina is constantly "cleaning up" the abusive messages on my social media accounts. But they keep popping up again and again. Then I forbid myself to read them.

There are three days left before my hotel lease expires. I have to decide what to do next. I am alone in a foreign country with no family, no home, no job, and no prospects.

"When are you coming home?" My daughter's voice on the phone is like a straw for a drowning man.

I talk to Arisha almost every day, and every time, I have to steel myself so she wouldn't feel my confusion. For her, I have to remain strong and confident. Without her knowing it, my little girl kept me afloat like no one else.

But now my strength is running out.

"I'm afraid to go back to Russia," I begin, frightened by my own frankness. "They might put me in jail. Wait a little longer; I'm thinking of a way to get you to Germany."

"There's no way my dad is going to let me go. He put a travel ban on me. I don't even have a passport."

"Arisha, we'll think of something. You know that there are no hopeless situations. We will definitely find a way out."

Through a secure messenger, I send endless messages to people I trust: "Help me get my daughter out of Russia." My friends helplessly shake their heads.

Suggestions to kidnap my daughter and take her out in the trunk of a car or take her across the border on someone else's passport are immediately rejected.

The phone rings.

"Hi! Everything is brilliantly simple." I hear the cheerful voice of a neighbor in our cottage community on the phone. "I found a firm in Moscow that will make a passport for a child without the presence of parents for forty thousand. All you need is a birth certificate and a residence registration document."

I'm almost dancing. For the first time in my life, I am glad that corruption is in full bloom in Russia.

In the evening I go out for a walk through the center of Berlin. I walk along Friedrichstrasse, breathing in the fresh air. Due to the events of the last few days, I no longer have the energy for a traditional jog. I'm looking at the faces of passersby. I see a lot of women with children. They laugh and excitedly tell each other something. I look at them with envy. Their lives seem happy and measured, planned out for years to come. But I do not know how and where I will live tomorrow. Each new day brings new problems that require immediate solutions. But I think I'm in luck. Arisha will soon be with me and we'll be able to stroll along Friedrichstrasse just as carefree!

"Can you imagine they turned me down? They just entered Arisha's data into the computer, and it immediately showed a mark—under the supervision of the FSB." A neighbor just stunned me with this message. No amount of money is going to help here.

The last hope I had has melted away. Now I have no choice but to go back. Everyone I tell about my plans unanimously tries to talk me out of it. They're sure I'll never get out of jail.

"Your passport seems to have been revoked," Savely says over the phone cheerfully, as always. Immediately after our meeting in Odesa, he left for Italy with his family.

"On what grounds? I am a citizen of Russia, so I have the right to enter. There are no criminal cases against me. So they will let me in freely and continue to play conspiracy games, if they want to. During this time, I'll solve my problems, sell my car, get my daughter a passport, and then I'll leave with her."

"You're taking a big risk. Okay, tell me your date of birth and the exact time you were born. I'll look up your horoscope."

Savely used to be a media manager and now he is a professional astrologer. Among his clients are major businessmen and even politicians. I don't believe in horoscopes, but I send him the data just in case. The next day, Savely sends me a voice message.

"I checked everything' there's no jail in your horoscope. But still, be careful. If they tell you your passport's been revoked and they put you on a bench in the terminal, then you sit and wait. And especially don't show off there...."

After listening to the message, I smile for the first time in days. Savely knows how to lighten the mood. I promise him I won't show off, though I'm not going to keep my mouth shut.

I spend the night before my flight at Brandenburg Airport. My hotel had run out of room, and I couldn't find another place to stay. The city is packed to capacity. There are a lot of refugees from Ukraine and the Russians who fled from Putin. There are almost no openings at cheap hotels. I make several attempts to book a hotel without a bank card, but this is not possible. None of my cards work outside of Russia due to sanctions. I understand everything; sanctions are a very effective measure to stop the war, so I just decide that I will sleep at the airport tonight.

I choose a free bench, sit down, put my head on my suitcase, and try to sleep. I have nightmares.

I dream about the Malaysian Boeing Flight MH-17. A family from Australia is walking among the wreckage of the plane. The spouses are looking for their only daughter. They say she wanted to go to Mars and change life for the better.

On that fateful day, July 17, 2014, when separatists shot down a Boeing passenger jet in Donbass, I was at work. It was evening prime time. All the management was in place, so decisions were made at lightning speed. There was no footage from the crash site yet, the black boxes had not been deciphered, but the culprits had already been found. Everything had to be blamed on Ukraine.

The first version of what happened was announced forty minutes after the crash in Vecherniye Novosti. A correspondent based in Donetsk reported that "a Ukrainian SU fighter jet attacked a passenger plane near the city of Snezhnoye and shot it down."

On the program *Vremya*, the military expert said very convincingly that: "It was possible to shoot down the airliner only from the Buk surface-to-air missile system, which the Ukrainian army has in service. The rebels have no such weapons...."

Toward the end, Ekaterina Andreeva reported: "The probable target of the Ukrainian missile could have been the plane of the President of Russia. On the right of full confidentiality, a source in Rosaviatsiya reported that Russian Air Force One and the Malaysian Boeing crossed at the same point and at the same echelon. It happened near Warsaw."

Disinformation was thrown in so professionally and convincingly that sometimes it seemed to me that not everything was so clear-cut. Imagine what the ordinary viewers who sat on the other side of the screen thought. The more unbelievable the lie, the more readily it was believed.

Eight years later, the District Court in The Hague considered all Russian versions and found them invalid. The international investigation team proved that the Malaysian Boeing had been shot down by a Buk surface-to-air missile system, which had been brought from Russia and then taken back. Three separatists were found guilty and sentenced in absentia to life imprisonment.

With a shudder, I wake up. I have a splitting headache. I get up and walk to the boarding gate. I realize that it would be a real ordeal for me to return to Russia. But there is no other way.

CHAPTER 19

RETURN TO RUSSIA

JULY 2022, MOSCOW

As soon as my plane lands at Vnukovo Airport, I call my new lawyer. Dmitry Zakhvatov is waiting for me in the arrivals hall.

"Give me your geolocation immediately," Dmitry advises. "If you get detained, I'll know where they're taking you."

After sending the geolocation, I call my daughter.

"Finally, you have arrived!" I hear her joyful voice. "When Dad found out that you were arriving, he quickly took me out of the house and hid me at my grandmother's in the country. But I don't want to sit here; take me away from here."

I walk resolutely toward passport control. The border guard looks at my passport.

"Step aside. We'll call you," he says.

I sit down on the bench and wait, as Savely advised. I notice that my phone's battery is rapidly dying because of geolocation. I scold myself for not buying a power bank and secretly hope that the battery can last until my meeting with the lawyer.

Footsteps are heard from the side. A man in plain clothes hands me my passport.

"You can go."

Without asking too many questions, I quickly pick up my suitcase and leave for the arrivals hall.

"Fire! They let you go!" the lawyer exclaims. Dmitry Zakhvatov is a tall, imposing man, young, but already a well-known human rights activist in Russia. Among his clients are members of Pussy Riot and several civil activists. While I was in Germany, he agreed to help me with a lawsuit related to my children.

"Haha, wait; it's not evening yet," I say ironically. "You think it's that easy? Now there's going to be some provocation."

As soon as I say this, we are blocked by an annoying tabloid reporter.

"How does it feel to return to the country from which you fled? How do you live when both Russians and Ukrainians hate you?"

I turn away from the camera and quicken my pace. I do not intend to answer provocative questions, because I am in the lair of the enemy. Now any of my words can be taken out of context and used against me. A reporter runs after us and films everything on his phone. He is only a step behind us. We jump in the car and lock all the doors.

"I hope we're not being followed." Dmitry looks intently into the rearview mirror as our car pulls out onto the Kiev highway. "They use gray cars for surveillance, some inconspicuous Ladas, Renaults, Chevrolets."

We do not notice anything suspicious. In the flow of cars we occasionally come across cars with the ominous letter Z. At the edges of the road there are billboards with pictures of men in military uniforms and the inscription, "Proud of the heroes!" Only the faces of these "heroes" are no fun at all. No one in their homeland greets them with flowers and honors.

We reach my community and drive up to my house. On the next street, a red banner with the USSR inscription is developing.

"It looks like my neighbor has decided, along with Putin, to go back to the time of the Soviet Union."

"Look." Dmitry points to another house. "And there's a pirate flag hanging here."

"When I left Moscow, this was not the case." Apparently, this was a way for a man to express his disagreement with what was going on. No wonder the war in Russia splits families apart. It seems that neighbors have stopped communicating with each other.

Dmitry sighs sadly, takes my suitcase out of the trunk, and leaves.

I go into the yard and see my mother.

"Oh, you are back! Who would have thought?" she says with indignation. "Why didn't you say anything when Yugoslavia was bombed? Or when the Ukrainian Nazis were destroying Russians in Donbass?"

My throat is constricting. I am very tired and decide to be silent. My mother, who is the same age as Putin, is zombified by Kremlin propaganda like millions of Russians. From morning till night she listens to Vladimir Solovyov, Putin's chief propagandist, who constantly substitutes concepts and teaches her to hate Ukrainians and Americans. He is the main authority for her. I am a nobody, a "fifth column" who is trying to destroy Russia. My attempts to bring the truth to my loved one are fruitless. Every conversation we have about politics inevitably ends in a fight.

I open the door. Two snow-white retrievers are literally bouncing up to the ceiling, licking my cheeks, whining and wagging their tails.

"Berry, I missed you, too." I scratch behind the ear of our beloved. And I'm amazed at how much her puppy has grown in these two months.

I hear my son's voice coming down from the second floor. "Well, at least you could have given me a warning that you were coming back."

"What's the problem?" I ask casually.

"Don't you want to live somewhere else? I'm worried about our safety. Why don't you rent an apartment?"

I try to explain to my son that I am not a criminal and I am not going to hide from anyone. I have my own house. And I'm tired of wandering around in hotels and other people's apartments.

"Then I'll go live with my father," he declares.

"Okay, it's your choice," I agree sadly, knowing full well that while I was away, my children were turned against me. It would be a while before it all falls into place.

As soon as I wake up, I go to court. There they have to determine with whom the children will live. As a rule, the courts in Russia leave the children with their mothers. But there are exceptions to every rule. My case is just like that.

There is a crowd of journalists outside the court building. But there is no opinion from the guardianship authorities in the case. The court session is postponed for almost three months.

My ex-spouse doesn't want to talk to me or my lawyer or journalists. He still hides my daughter from me. He is obviously following someone's orders from above. I can't find any other explanation for his actions. On his side are a gigantic propaganda machine Russia Today, power, and money. I understand that there is an unequal struggle ahead of me.

A week goes by, and then a second week. Like an enraged tigress, I rush around the house, calling my son, relatives, and friends, asking them to help me get my daughter back.

Arisha does not sit idly by either; she fights for her freedom. Ten times a day she calls her father at work. She demands, insists, pleads, cries, persuades, and finally begs. Under her pressure all obstacles collapse. A few days later, she appears on the doorstep of our house.

There is no limit to our happiness. We sit in the kitchen, joking and laughing. And we tell each other without stopping what we've been through.

It is at this point that a call from the Ministry of Internal Affairs comes in.

"You gave us the documents for your daughter's passport. But we can't make her a passport. It is forbidden for the child to travel abroad."

"I'm not going to take her abroad yet; I just want to get her paperwork done."

"No, we're not going to make her a passport."

"You have no right," I try to argue. "I will appeal. The other parent cannot be restricted in his or her rights if he or she is acting in the best interest of the child."

I hear muffled laughter on the other end of the line. And immediately I come down from heaven to earth. What appeal? There are no laws in Russia, especially against those who dared to speak out against the criminal war.

"Moscow Municipal Deputy Alexei Gorinov faces ten years in prison," I read in the news feed.

The politician was arrested because, at a meeting of the Council of Deputies, he proposed not to hold a children's drawing contest, but instead to honor the memory of the victims of the war in Ukraine. The "investigation" of this case took only five days, and the trial was immediately closed to the public.

Without thinking, I went to the Meshchansky court building to support Alexei. There is a crowd of the deputy's supporters in the street. No one is allowed inside. People are watching what is happening in the courtroom on the online broadcast.

In the crowd I recognize the young journalist Slava Tikhonov, who was fired from the TV channel Moscow 24 for asking motorists not to glue the letter *Z* on the back windows of cars on live TV.

"In recent months I have been working with politician Ilya Yashin," Slava explains to me, "but a few days ago he was also arrested and locked up for fifteen days, allegedly for disobeying the police. Most likely, a criminal case will also be opened against him. So I'm at a loss. I don't even know what I'm going to do next. Looks like I'll be out of a job again."

People who came to support the deputy start coming up to us.

"Anya", a short girl with dark, curly hair, introduces herself. "I hang green ribbons symbolizing peace around Moscow and put stickers saying, 'No to War.' I do this very carefully so that I don't get caught and go to jail like Sasha Skochilenko, who replaced the price tags in the supermarket with anti-war leaflets."

Six months later, the security forces break into Anya's apartment. And she will be forced to flee to Kazakhstan.

"Dmitri", her companion, a tall, thin, middle-aged man, introduces himself. "I am a neurosurgeon. I came to support Alexei Gorinov."

"Aren't you afraid that you will be fired?" I wonder. "You work in a state institution, don't you?"

"I don't give a damn about them! I'm not a slave but a free man," he answers proudly. "I'm actually from Crimea. Back in 2014, when Russia seized the peninsula, it was clear how it would end."

Not far from us is an elderly woman with short gray hair. She is dressed in an embroidered vest and has a canvas bag on her shoulder that reads, "No to War."

"I am a Muscovite with Ukrainian roots," she explains.

The police will grab her the very next day and try to push her into a police van. Dozens of people will stand up for her. They will literally snatch the courageous woman from the clutches of law enforcement officers.

While we are standing on the street, the absurd sentence of Alexei Gorinov is read out in the court building: "Motivated by political hatred...He cynically used his official position and disseminated knowingly false information about the activities of the Russian Armed Forces."

The defendant does not admit his guilt. He stands in a glass bowl and holds a piece of paper with the inscription: "Do you still need this war?"

"Seven years in jail," the judge says. Gorinov's wife gets hysterical right in the courtroom.

In the evening at home I could not find room for myself with impotent rage. Like millions of people in Russia, I am stunned by the new reality. Just now, acting cynically and brutally, the authorities have taken seven years of life from an innocent man. He is no longer young, and prison could kill him.

It was the first real prison sentence under the new criminal article on fakes. The more Russia lost in this war, the fiercer the political repression became.

Criminal charges were also filed against opposition politician Ilya Yashin, a longtime and consistent critic of Vladimir Putin. From day one, Ilya spoke out against the war and told Russians about the atrocities of Russian soldiers in Bucha, Irpen, and Mariupol. Despite numerous threats, he refused to leave Russia because he was genuinely worried about the future of his country.

Here is what Ilya said in one of his last broadcasts: "Whatever word Putin and his entourage use to cover these events, like a fig leaf, bashfully, not to call it a special operation or some other synonyms...denazification, demilitarization...this war, from the first moments it was clear that this is a war...millions of people are fleeing their homes in the hope of saving lives. A sea of blood, a sea of tears, and, unfortunately, there is no end in sight."

Dozens of Ilya Yashin's supporters have come to the Basmanny court building when the politician is being sentenced. The crowd is full of familiar faces.

"Why did you come to support Ilya Yashin?" a journalist asks me.

I reply, "Ilya Yashin is one of the most ambitious, young, and brightest politicians in Russia. The future belongs to people like Ilya Yashin; that's why I'm here. I came to support him; he needs our support right now. I think war is the worst crime of the twenty-first century. I firmly believe that the criminals who started the war will sit in the dock at the International Tribunal in the end, and what they are doing now in Ukraine is madness; it is a frantic attempt to keep power in their hands."

I see my acquaintances Anya and Dmitry, who came to support Alexei Gorinov at the Meshchansky Court a few days ago.

"Why are you talking so openly? The crowd is full of 'E' men," Anya asks me.

"Who are they?"

"Don't you know? These are officers from the Center for Countering Extremism, the so-called political police."

At that moment, a short young guy emerges from the crowd. He introduces himself as a journalist and starts asking provocative questions. I refuse to answer.

"Did you know that administrative proceedings were instituted against you for discrediting the army?" he asks in a cryptic tone and, without waiting for an answer, disappears into the crowd.

What does that mean? Immediately, I call my lawyer.

Dmitry Zakhvatov quickly double-checks the information. Indeed, the case was initiated after my post on social networks, published for *Russia Day*. In it, I wrote, "I have no reason to be proud of my country. Being a Russian is now a disgraceful stigma. Russia treacherously attacked an independent state under the cover of night and is destroying the Ukrainian people. It invades other people's territories instead of developing its own."

Near Basmanny Court, the police throw active supporters of Ilya Yashin into police vans and quickly take them away.

"Let's clear the sidewalk," the policeman shouts into the loudspeaker, trying to disperse the crowd.

"Freedom to him! Freedom to him!" the crowd chants as Ilya Yashin is taken out of the building and put into a truck.

A few months later, the court sentenced the politician to eight and a half years in prison.

CHAPTER 20
DETENTION

"Berry, Berry, let's go for a walk," I call to the dog.

Together with the puppy, she runs up to me, happily wagging her tail.

After putting on my shorts and sneakers, I go out, intending to take a walk in the nearby woods.

On the way out of the village, I meet a neighbor.

"Hey, how are you doing?" he asks me as he rides up to me on his bike.

Arthur[¶¶] comes from Central Asia but has lived in Moscow for a long time. I met him after my protest on live television. At a time when some of my friends and acquaintances had abruptly turned their backs on me, Arthur offered to help me. Before the war, he was trading with the New York Stock Exchange, but right after the sanctions were imposed, his business collapsed. Arthur was friends with Navalny's associates, and his messenger avatars read, "Russia will be free!"

"It's as good as it gets," I reply.

¶¶ Name changed

We go out the gates of the village together. Two policemen run up to me.

"Come with us," says one of them, pointing toward a white police van.

"What happened?" I am perplexed.

"All questions will be answered later."

A man in civilian clothes comes out of the minibus toward me.

"Do you have a passport?" he asks deliberately sternly.

His face is covered by a black mask and a dark cap on his head. He glares at me. Later I found out that he was an operative from the E Center who was always following me.

"Of course not. I don't walk my dogs with my passport. Can I go get my passport, change my clothes, and take the dogs back?"

"No, you're detained."

"Can I bring her passport?" Arthur asks.

"Bring it on."

"Arthur," I say to my neighbor, "the house is open. Mom is watering the flowers in the plot. My passport is in a white bag in the hallway on the dresser. There's also a sheet with all the phone numbers on it. The first one is Christina; call her. She knows everyone—my lawyer and all my friends. And please take the dogs home."

Berry, anticipating her separation, begins to whimper. She cannot understand what unknown force makes her rush home with a stranger.

"Go home, Berry. I'll be right back." I rub her ear.

Berry and her puppy reluctantly walk toward the house, following Arthur.

"Get in the car, turn off the phone, and put it on the table," the anti-extremism investigator commands.

I do what he says. The police don't notice the second phone. It is still in my pocket. After a while my neighbor brings my passport. The police car pulls out onto the Kievskoe highway and moves toward the center. The anti-extremism investigator sits in the front, and in front of me there are two policemen. All the way there they keep an eye on me.

On the light-colored car blind hangs two badges. One has a portrait of the murdered politician Boris Nemtsov on it, and the other has the inscription, "No to War!"

"It's funny. You arrested me for my anti-war stance, and you have a 'No War!' badge hanging in your car," I remark in surprise.

"We confiscated this from the detainees," the policeman replies dryly.

Our car has been looping through the streets of the city for two hours now.

"Where are you taking me? Can I call my lawyer?"

"No," replies the masked man sharply. "Why do you dislike your homeland so much?"

"I love my homeland; it's just that criminals have seized power in it," I retort.

"You are the criminal. People like you should be in prison. You are destroying our country. Ukraine must not join NATO; otherwise the alliance will be at our borders."

"If you are fighting NATO, you have already lost. Sweden and Finland, which until now had maintained neutral status, want to join NATO because of the war. Now Russia has a huge common border with the North Atlantic Alliance."

"It sounds like you work for the CIA and NATO."

"I've been accused of a lot of things. I was simply expressing my civic position. You have intimidated the entire population of Russia; people are so afraid that they keep quiet like slaves. Why do you hide your face under a mask? Are you ashamed of your work? It's on your conscience that hundreds of innocent people have been tortured."

The anti-extremism investigator's mouth is filled with foul language. He starts using psychological pressure, accusing me of working for Western intelligence services.

I start coughing nervously again. I turn to the window and shut up. I don't want to have another useless dialogue with the chain dog and faithful guard of Putin's criminal regime. The car pulls up to a small two-story police station. They take me inside the building.

"I have to go to the bathroom," I say and head resolutely toward the door with the sign "W."

One of the policemen rushes after me. In the booth I take out my second phone and quickly type a message to my lawyer. He is looking for me all over Moscow. My excitement makes my fingers slip over the touchscreen, and I don't hit the letters.

"Krasnoseiski ovd," I misspell and quickly press the Send button.

In just a few minutes, Dmitry Zakhvatov rushed to the police station.

"They charged you under an administrative article for discrediting the army. Specifically, they didn't like the interview you gave to journalists outside the Basmanny Court when Yashin was on trial," the lawyer says.

"It's clear that this is my second administrative case under an unconstitutional article. They are trying to silence me."

We go outside. It is drizzling. The lawyer's phone is ringing off the hook with calls from journalists.

"Are you going to comment on anything?" Dmitry asks.

"No, the detention was so unexpected. Honestly, I was nervous and cold and very tired. Call me a cab."

In the middle of the night, when everyone is already asleep, I go home.

In a few days Russian courts will find me guilty in two administrative cases. I am given large fines for allegedly discrediting the Russian army with my words.

In the evening, my daughter and I are sitting in the kitchen. Her summer vacation is rapidly approaching its end. This year, for the first time, we could not go to the sea. All of our plans for the summer were ruined by the war. But most of my former TV colleagues continued to pretend that nothing was going on. I open up social media, and their happy faces would flash before me, with them enjoying a vacation somewhere in the Arab Emirates or the Maldives. I systematically deleted these people from my social networks, marveling at their cynicism. It seemed to me that any normal person's life should be divided into *before* and *after* the war began.

My daughter's voice interrupted my musings.

"Let's make pizza in the oven for dinner."

"That's a great idea," I say and look in the fridge. "There are tomatoes, sausage, cheese, and olives, too."

Berry comes to the table and looks into my eyes, wagging her tail. I cut off a piece of sausage and hand it to the dog. She swallows it instantly.

I cut the tomatoes; my daughter spreads them on the dough. After all the trials that have befallen us, we are finally together.

At the same time, Russian troops are shelling Vinnitsa. One of the shells hit the center of the city. More than twenty civilians were killed, among them four-year-old Liza, a sunny child. Her tiny body was torn apart by a shell right in the stroller, and her mother's leg was torn off.

In the evening I read about this tragedy in the news.

I am overwhelmed with a feeling of helplessness and despair. Who will give this little girl back to her mother? Who will give the parents back their dead children?

The next day I decide to go on a solitary picket.

"Don't go, don't go; they'll arrest you," Christina shouts into the phone.

"They're allowed to kill children, and I'm not even allowed to go out on a solitary picket," I shout back. "Silence is complicity in crimes. Solitary pickets are not forbidden in Russia."

"Well, I know you can't be convinced. I'll go with you."

Christina was in Moscow at the time. She had flown in from Samara with her girlfriends, having taken an unscheduled vacation. The large logistics company she worked for was on the verge of bankruptcy due to the imposition of sanctions. There were almost no orders.

"If you're in Moscow, come to me," I suggest.

Just an hour later, a frail, pretty, medium-sized girl with straight blond hair and round glasses shows up on my doorstep. For the first time, we see each other in real life, not on a smartphone screen. My daughter has a special connection with Christina from the first moment she sees her.

The next day, together with Christina, we get in a cab to make it harder for the cameras to track us, and we rush to the Kremlin. On Sophia's embankment, I unfold a banner with pictures of children killed in Ukraine. Lonely passersby stare at the inscription: "Putin is a murderer! His soldiers are fascists! 352 children have died. How many more children must die for you to stop?"

There are bloody dolls lying at my feet.

Fifteen minutes pass. Several policemen head in our direction across Nemtsov Bridge.

"Let's get out of here; we can't take that risk." Christina worries.

She calls a cab. A couple of minutes later a yellow Kia stops in front of us. I jump in the car and dial the number of my lawyer. I explain what is going on.

"Quickly, come to my house," Dmitry says without hesitation.

Together with Christina, I go to his small apartment.

"Fire!" admires Dmitry. "Well, you're on a roll! For these times, it's very brave."

We spend a few more hours together with the lawyer and his family. Closer to midnight I tell Dmitry I'm going home.

"Christina will go with me. If anything happens to me, Christina will call you."

"All right. And don't go beyond the gates of the village again," Dmitry warns.

Two days later, I notice surveillance. Outside the gates of the village on a vacant lot is a gray Lada with two men in it.

I call my lawyer to tell him.

"There's some suspicious gray car outside the village gate. Can you check it out?"

I dictate the number. After a few minutes, Dmitry calls back.

"Yes, that's them."

I walk up to the guard of our cottage community, who is sitting in a small iron hut near the barrier.

"Do you know what kind of suspicious car is behind the gate?"

"They've been standing here for two days on duty. The cars keep changing. They're watching you, Marina Vladimirovna." The guard grins. "I went up to them and asked."

At this point, the lawyer calls again.

"You want to laugh? The mother of one of my defendants, when he was under surveillance, used to come to these guys and bring them food."

"Haha, I can only bring these bums cockroach poison pies," I joke bitterly. "I have to go to the center of Moscow tomorrow. I arranged to meet with German journalists."

"Be careful. If anything happens, call me right away."

In the morning I call a cab and drive to the subway. As soon as we leave the cottage village, a gray SUV with mud-covered license plates jumps out from behind the garages and tails us. The cab stops by the subway, and so does the SUV. I run into the subway, and the passenger in the SUV follows me.

I sit down and start reading a book. I physically feel the presence of a stranger next to me, who glares at me.

Don't think about him, I tell myself. *You're not going to do anything wrong; let him go if he has to.*

"Next station Park Kultury!" announces the loudspeaker.

I jump out of the train, and a man in unremarkable gray clothes follows me. I move to the escalator to make a change. I involuntarily look back; the stranger is a few meters away from me. I feel uncomfortable. I abruptly stop right in front of the escalator and walk against the crowd. The man does not have time to react, and the flow of people picks him up and carries him up the escalator. He follows me with a long look.

I understand that I got away from demonstrative surveillance, but it's too early to rejoice. Now, they will follow me on cameras. For the last few years, Moscow has been running a state-of-the-art facial recognition system called Sphere. It was with the help of this system that the police detained politician Leonid Gozman, a longtime enemy of Putin, in the subway. First, a case was brought against the oppositionist for failing to notify him of dual citizenship; then there were two administrative arrests for posts on social networks. Gozman was held for thirty days in a special detention center and then left Russia.

I get out of the subway and walk along the embankment to Nemtsov Bridge, to the very spot where I stood in a solitary picket. A film crew from Germany is waiting for me there. We're starting to record the interview. Immediately a detachment of police officers appears near us.

"Watching you," says the German reporter.

"Let them watch. I have nothing to hide. This is a method of psychological pressure."

The police officers defiantly approach us and start checking our documents. After writing down the data of my companions, they quietly disappear.

CHAPTER 21

A NIGHT IN JAIL

A dog barks loudly on the first floor of the house in the pre-dawn silence. I jump out of bed.

"Berry, what happened?"

The dog does not stop barking. I pull back the heavy curtain and look out the window. About a dozen men in blue camouflage stand near my fence. Several men in plain clothes are walking quickly toward my house. Everything inside me shatters.

"Open up," comes a shout, followed by a demanding knock on the door.

I pull on my pants and T-shirt and run down the stairs. Christina peeks out of the next room, her hair tangled from sleep, a black headband on her forehead. Her vacation is coming to an end; in three days she has to leave for Samara.

"Quick, call my lawyer," I tell her. "Ask him what we should do. I'm afraid they're going to burst into the house and scare Arisha." My daughter is sound asleep in her room and doesn't hear loud noises.

Someone downstairs is banging on the door with their fist. "Open up! Immediately! We have a search warrant."

"Can I call my lawyer?" I ask.

"If you don't open now, we'll start sawing locks," replies a rough male voice.

I look through the peephole. On the threshold is a man in the uniform of an employee of the Ministry of Emergency Situations. He is holding a grinder.

I quickly swing the door open. About a dozen employees burst into the house. Among them I recognize the operative from the E Center who supervised me. He is still hiding his face under a black mask.

"I'm begging you, just don't scare my daughter! She's still asleep!"

"You are being searched under criminal article 207.3 part two on the distribution of knowingly false information about the Russian army," says a young man in a gray suit. "I am an investigator for particularly important cases of the IC (Investigative Committee). Go ahead."

The last phrase, or rather, the order, is addressed to two men in plain clothes. They, like hungry bloodhounds and begin to examine the contents of all the cupboards.

"Why don't you wait for the lawyer? He'll be here in an hour," Christina asks, coming down from the second floor.

"We won't wait for anyone," the investigator replies firmly.

"What are you looking for? Maybe I can help you?" I ask them delicately.

"We need all your gadgets," replies the operative.

"Here's my phone." I voluntarily give them my old Samsung.

"Whose iPhone is that?" the operative exclaims, looking at my iPhone on the bedside table.

I look away. Christina comes to the rescue. She leaps forward sharply. "That's my iPhone!"

"Enter the password." The operative is not going to take her word for it.

Christina easily enters the password because she knows all the passwords for my phones and social networks, which I myself regularly forget.

"Okay," the masked man says doubtfully and gives her the iPhone. "Take it."

We smile imperceptibly at each other. It was a miracle that Christina managed to save my iPhone. We knew perfectly well that all the equipment that fell into the hands of the police disappeared forever. It was impossible to get it back.

It is the second hour of the search. I quietly go into my daughter's room. She is sitting on the bed and crying.

"Why are you crying? We're being searched. But don't worry; they won't go into your room yet."

"I'm not afraid. I just got a call from Kirill, and he said he was coming to take me to Daddy. I don't want to go to Daddy," Arisha whispers through her tears, sobbing. "Mom, I want to be here with you and Christina."

"Don't cry; everything will be all right," I comfort her.

An hour later, my son appears on the doorstep.

"What's going on here?"

"Search. You know everything from the internet; that's why Dad sent you here."

"Arisha, come with me," Kirill says sternly to Arisha. "Children don't belong here."

"I don't want to." My daughter sobs.

He abruptly grabs his little sister's hand and leads her to the door. I stare sadly in their wake. The war destroyed millions of families, not only in Ukraine but also in Russia. People close to each other could go months without speaking to each other.

"Kiryusha, it's okay." I try to start a conversation with my son, though I know this is not a good time for that. "Now the cops will be gone, and everything will be as it was before. You'd better stay home with your sister."

"No, nothing will ever be the same again," he says sternly and walks out the door with Arisha.

It is now the seventh hour of the search. One of the police officers notices the entrance to the attic. I explain to them that I'm storing old things there after I moved. They climb into the attic.

Having found an old system unit there, the police take it downstairs. After making an inventory of the seized equipment, the investigator tells me to get in the car:

"Let's go to the Investigative Committee."

"Can I come with you?" Christina asks timidly.

The investigator nods.

We sit in the back seat of the car.

"Give me the phone," I whisper.

Christina quietly hands me the rescued iPhone. I open my social media and quickly type a message about my arrest.

"That was quick," says the black-masked anti-extremism officer riding in the car with us. He was constantly monitoring my social media and now he realizes he made a mistake.

"Get out of the car," he says sharply to Christina.

She is forced to submit.

The police car pulls into the territory of the Investigative Committee. There I meet my lawyer Dmitry Zakhvatov. Together with the investigator and the anti-extremism officer, we go up to the fifth floor.

The interrogation continues for several hours.

"If you don't want to answer the questions, you can refer to Article 51 of the Constitution," the lawyer advises me.

"I know, but I don't deny the fact that I protested on the Sofia embankment."

"You know," I say to the investigator, "I cried when I was putting pictures of children killed in Ukraine on the poster. For the rest of my life I will remember an interview with Sergey, which I accidentally saw on CNN back in the early days of the war. He was telling the anchor, Erin Burnett, that he lost his entire family in Irpen—his wife and two children. The CNN anchor was crying in the frame. I was sobbing behind the scenes. His son and daughter were the same age as mine. Do you have families? Can you imagine yourself in Sergey's shoes?"

The investigator lowers his eyes. An oppressive silence reigns in the office. Even the cynical officer from the E Center and the two police officers sitting in the corner of the office are sullenly silent.

After the interrogation, the operatives take me to the courtyard of the Investigative Committee. A paddy wagon pulls up there. I am handcuffed.

"They're taking you to the temporary detention center in Petrovka," the lawyer shouts to me as we leave.

The door slams shut. I'm alone in a tiny cage. I sink down on the bench, staring out the small, barred window with a glassy eye. After half an hour, the van pulls up in front of the detention center.

The young warden on duty that night comes out to meet me. She looks at the new inmate with surprise. My white pantsuit is clearly dissonant with the prison bunk.

"I can't deviate from the rules. We have a standard procedure here," she says in a curt voice as if apologizing.

The warden quickly leads me into an iron cage and locks me up.

After taking off the handcuffs, she shouts, "Take off all your jewelry, earrings, rings, and take off your clothes. I need to search you."

After subjecting me to a humiliating procedure, she starts going through my things in my bag.

"You can't use that; you can't use that either," she says, putting aside the contents of my makeup bag.

After gutting my bag, the warden commands, "Out! Right, face the wall, now left and up the stairs. Wait, turn and face the wall!"

With a deafening screech, the thick iron door opens. I step into the unknown. There is no one inside the cell. The strong smell of urine hits my nose. Behind a small partition in the corner of the room there is a lavatory and next to it, a small washbasin. The walls of the room are painted dark green; the paint is cracked and peeling in some places.

I unwrap the thin gray mattress and lie down on the bed. A black peephole of a video camera stares at me from the ceiling. Heavy footsteps are heard behind the door, and someone's eye is fixed on the observation hole. I close my eyes and fall into an anxious half-forgetfulness. A terrible picture from my distant youth comes to mind. I was a young journalist who had come to the prison to record an interview with a serial killer.

2001, NOVOROSSIYSK MAXIMUM SECURITY PRISON.

"Yes, I killed them! I had to check whether I was a man or a creature," the gray-robed murderer whispered ominously into my microphone, his toothless mouth twitching.

In the late nineties, he formed a gang that killed people and stole their cars. The ringleader had at least seven victims on his conscience. He was sentenced to life in prison.

While in prison, the killer did not repent but rather tried to impose his philosophy on others, which made the blood in our veins run cold. We recorded the interview in a separate cell, separated from the serial killer by an iron bar.

"What is human life, just trash. It's worthless," the killer said, clearly enjoying the attention.

With my eyes wide open, I, a very young woman, listened to his monologue. I couldn't get a word out. I was not prepared for such a provocative interview. At one point the distraught inmate suddenly jumped up toward the bars, grabbed the microphone, and jerked it violently toward him. I recoiled in horror. Two guards jumped up to the murderer and handcuffed him.

"The interview is over. Leave the premises!" shouted the warden anxiously.

At that moment, I wake up from a coughing fit. A sticky sweat covers my whole body. A dim lamp burns on the ceiling, and I stare at one point, trying to understand how, twenty years later, I found myself inside the exact same prison cell into which murderers, rapists, and robbers used to be thrown. How did I end up here?

Why are dozens of innocent politicians and journalists who wanted the best for their country languishing in prison or in exile? And the real criminals, murderers, rapists, and looters who are destroying the population of Ukraine are still at large? I ask myself these questions and find no answers. Russia had become a country where absolute evil triumphed at that moment.

The bright light hits my eyes. It's still dark outside, but the lights in the cell have been turned on.

"Get up and make your bed!" The warden's voice comes from outside the door. I slowly sit up on the bed, remembering that I was promised a 6:00 a.m. wake-up call. My head splits open with pain. There is a loud clang of keys in the keyhole.

"Go out!" shouts the elderly warden, her face twisted with anger at such an early hour in the morning. "Get your things and come out! Hands forward!" she commands and snaps the handcuffs on my wrists. "Go to the right, facing the wall, go out into the corridor!"

She leads me into the next cell. In a thick veil of tobacco smoke sits a flabby woman. Her arms are tattooed.

"Hi, my name is Galya. I'm from Novorossiysk." She turns to me. "I just arrived in Moscow two days ago, and the mysora (dismissive name of the policemen) picked me up right away. I did sixteen years before that. I killed two men. Fuck them; it's their own fault. They shouldn't have gotten involved...."

"And now why have they brought you here?" I am timidly curious.

"I also stabbed a man with a knife in Novorossiysk, and I came here to Moscow, thinking that I could hide here."

"Didn't you know that Moscow has the most advanced facial recognition system?" I ask. "Video cameras are everywhere; not even a mouse can get by unnoticed here."

"Who knew." My cellmate waves her hand bitterly.

Galya smokes nervously and swears incessantly. Constantly coughing and panting, I try not to pass out. At that moment, my strongest desire is to take a breath of fresh air.

"What's the matter with you? You're not used to it, are you? If you end up in a pre-trial detention center, there are forty people sitting in one cell and almost all of them smoke. Why were you brought here?" Galya asks.

"For being against the war and asking not to kill children."

"What the fuck is going on?" Galya is swearing again. "I'm against the war, too. They're fucking crazy. People go to jail for that! What's going on? Children are sacred. I'd kill for my kids...."

At that moment the door opens. The jailer pushes a fragile young girl who looks about twenty-five years old into the cell. Like a frightened little deer, she sits silently on the bed and, without answering any questions, cries silently. I can see that she is in deep shock. I try to calm her down, but she cries even harder.

It's getting close to lunchtime.

"Ovsyannikova, get dressed and come out!" The warden's gruff voice booms. "Now you are going to the Basmanny Court."

As soon as I heard the name of the court, all hopes for a fair verdict dissipated like smoke. The Basmanny Court has been a symbol of political repression in Russia since the trial of Mikhail Khodorkovsky, the owner of Yukos. Because of his political ambitions, he was put behind bars for eleven years. It was after the Yukos case that the term "Basmanny Justice" was coined in Russia to refer to a corrupt court, which, at the order of the authorities, passed unjust verdicts.

The warden takes me back into the iron cage and searches me. In a pile of paper, she accidentally finds a piece of paper that reads, "Let the dead children haunt you in your dream." She quickly grabs it, crumples it, and tosses it in the trash. Sitting in a shaking bus, I remember the torn body of a four-year-old girl, Liza from Vinnitsa, and write these words over and over and over again...

The car stops at the Basmanny Court. It's a small old two-story building in the center of Moscow. Two guards lead me in from the back entrance and throw me into a tiny cell somewhere in the basement.

"They're going to come and search you again," says one of the guards.

"How many times can you search me? Are you kidding me?" I'm indignant.

The door closes with a rattle. Pulling two folded white pieces of paper from my pocket that read, "Let the dead children haunt you in your dream," I frantically figure out where to hide them. I tuck one into the sleeve of my jacket and the other into my sandals. The blood pulses in my temples; my heart is pounding frantically. The search could begin at any minute.

When the female guard with the metal detector appears at the door of the cell, I start coughing nervously again. She looks at me lazily and moves the metal detector in front of me. The paper, fortunately, does not trigger it.

I have been sitting in the basement of the Basmanny Court for more than five hours. They constantly bring new defendants to my cell; after some time, they are taken away, and new ones are brought in. Finally, toward the evening, the door opens and four huge guards in black masks appear on the threshold.

"Come out," says one of them. "Let's go up to the second floor."

Handcuffed, I am led through a crowd of journalists. The main thing I'm thinking about at this moment is that my children are about to see these videos, and they will be in for a real shock. Will I ever be able to explain to them that their mother, like dozens of other political prisoners in Russia, is not a criminal?

I am led into a glass aquarium. I've only seen these in movies before.

My lawyer walks up to the thick glass. "It's okay; the prosecutor wants to put you under house arrest! I was sure they would throw you in the detention center," Dmitry Zakhvatov tells me, smiling.

"Thank God!" I exclaim joyfully.

After a night spent in the detention center, I am well aware that I would not have survived in the detention center. I would have broken down or fallen into a depression.

Judge Natalia Dudar, who previously tried politicians Alexei Navalny and Ilya Yashin, declares the hearing on the preventive measure closed to the public.

"What are you afraid of?" I exclaim. "We need to make the process as open as possible. Even in the Soviet Union cases for anti-Soviet propaganda and dissemination of knowingly false information denigrating the Soviet system were considered openly."

Such arguments have no effect on the judge. She is simply carrying out an order from the Kremlin. All trials under the new article on fakes must be held behind closed doors.

Before the session begins, several accredited journalists are allowed into the room. I quickly unfold a piece of paper with the inscription "Let the dead children haunt you in your dream" and put it against the glass. Two guards, like huge gorillas, jump to the glass fence, their arms and bodies trying to shield the sheet of paper from the journalists.

"Get the press out. Let's go, let's go," one of them shouts.

Cameras flash. Four policemen quickly push the reporters out of the hall. As soon as the door closes behind the reporters, one of the policemen walks into my cage and quickly snatches the piece of paper.

Next they bring in a second group of reporters. Among them, I notice a familiar cameraman from Agence France Press. In front of his video camera, I quickly unfold a second sheet of paper with the same phrase. Everything repeats the familiar scenario. The guards immediately push the French man out the door.

"You are being guarded even more than Chikatilo (Soviet serial killer)," remarks my lawyer.

"Of course, a piece of paper in modern Russia has become more dangerous than a gun," I shout from the glass tank.

Journalists are no longer allowed in the hall. The judge hurriedly starts reading out the charges. The investigation believes that acting on the grounds of political hatred and hostility, I disseminated knowingly false information about the Russian army. According to the prosecutor, the data about 352 children killed in Ukraine doesn't correspond to reality. During special military operations, the Russian Ministry of Defense launches high-precision strikes and does not report the deaths of children. The judge gives me the floor.

"Dear judge, do you think that the death of children during the war is fake? Let's look at the UN statistics. You can go to the UN website—it is not blocked in Russia—and look, it says everything. All cases have been documented by international experts who worked at the crime scenes, as well as by employees of the Prosecutor General's Office of Ukraine. At the trial, we will present video evidence of the deaths of Ukrainian children. I will record an interview with their parents. There is no need for you to put me under house arrest because I am not guilty of anything."

But the judge remains adamant. Late at night a Federal Penitentiary Service car comes to pick me up. I will spend the next two months under house arrest without access to a telephone or the Internet.

CHAPTER 22
FAMILY DRAMA

It is almost midnight on the clock. An officer of the Investigative Committee is diligently writing something in his report. And the FSIN inspector walks around my house and sets up base stations in every room, looking like old bulky phones. These devices have only buttons for emergency assistance and communication with the FSIN.

The inspector snaps an electronic bracelet on my leg that looks a lot like a fitness tracker.

"What principle does it work on?"

"The bracelet constantly transmits a signal to the base stations," the inspector explains, "so if you leave the house, we'll know about it immediately. And then you'll get a tougher sentence."

Christina suddenly appears on my doorstep. I am insanely happy to see her. I can't even believe that she managed to fly to Samara so quickly, quit her job, and come back.

"Can I work as a food delivery boy?" smiling and a little flirtatious, Christina asks, dropping two heavy bags of groceries on the floor.

"Actually, the ruling of the Basmanny Court says that Marina Vladimirovna can communicate only with her lawyer and close relatives," the employee of the Investigative Committee mouths in a monotone. "Are you a relative of hers?"

"No, I'm her friend," Christina answers, smiling, trying to pretend that nothing special is going on. "Marina has no relatives who can take care of her," Christina explains. "Her mother wants Marina to go to jail as soon as possible because she is against Putin. And her adult son has left home. I'm the only one who can help her."

"Indeed," I confirm. "Without Christina's help, I would starve to death under house arrest. Even in pretrial detention facilities, prisoners are cooked and brought food."

The investigator is thinking hard. The clock reads almost midnight. He is tired and really wants to go home. Ultimately he decides that he will deal with the problem later and leaves.

A few days later he calls me in for questioning.

After breaking out of my confinement for a while, I look around the sides of the road with interest.

"How many prisoners do you have like me?"

"You're the first one we've had under a political article," explains the FSIN inspector. "Usually we have crooks and drug addicts under house arrest. In that house," the inspector points to a gray apartment building, "there was a man who formed a gang of car thieves. And in that one—" he waves his hand in the direction of the neighboring five-story building "—there was a woman who stabbed her husband in the heat of a family quarrel."

My interlocutor averts his eyes embarrassedly to the side and quietly utters a phrase that sticks in my memory for a long time: "The most important thing is not to worry, Marina; we all love you and support you."

Suddenly I am embarrassed and at a loss for words. But why do people, who know perfectly well that this system is completely rotten, continue to carry out its criminal orders? The inspector of the FSIN seems to be a decent man, and he is troubled by remorse. At least he knows that my arrest was illegal. I wonder if the judge, who ordered me under house arrest at the order of the authorities, feels anything like that? And the investigator who fabricated the criminal case against me? And the ex-spouse who works for the Kremlin and participates in my harassment?

The summer is coming to an end. Three weeks have passed since my arrest, and I haven't seen my daughter all this time. I could not leave the house by order of the Basmanny Court, and my daughter could not leave the apartment by order of her father.

"Your house is a prison now! And you won't see your mother again," her father told Arisha after they put an electronic bracelet on me. He locked the child in his apartment and forbade her to communicate with me.

Every day I think painfully about the precious time we are losing. Maybe, very soon, I will be sent to a detention center, and then I really won't be able to see my daughter. I will spend at least five years in prison, or even longer if the authorities want to give me a trial. When I get out, Arisha will be all grown up; she will graduate from high school and prepare to go to university. Time is running out; we have to act, but my hands are helplessly tied. I can barely control my tears. I try to distract myself from my sad thoughts.

"Don't worry; everything will be fine," Christina encourages me. "We'll figure something out. Her dad has forbidden Arisha to talk to me, too. She sneaks me letters, misses you very much, and wants to come home."

I miss my daughter, too. The days under house arrest drag on unbearably slowly. The summer vacations are over, and school is due to start in a day. But I sit alone, locked in four walls.

Suddenly there is a quiet knock on the door. Frightened, I freeze for a moment and listen.

"Mommy, it's me," my daughter's voice comes to me.

I open the door quickly. Arisha, shaking with fear, throws herself around my neck. Her knees are trembling, and so are her hands.

"Mommy, I downloaded the app and called a cab when Daddy left for work and Kirill went out to the store," she says excitedly, rushing to tell me everything. "They called me a hundred times while I was in the cab, screaming, texting me to come back immediately."

"It's okay; you're with your mom," I reassure the child, and at the same time I'm amazed at her courage.

Arisha continues to shake. I realize that my hugs and words are not enough, so I take a tablet of valerian from the medicine cabinet and pour her a glass of water.

"Drink this; you need to calm down."

"In general, I'm a free person, and my home is not a prison. Besides, from the age of ten, children can decide for themselves who they want to live with," Arisha declares a bit later.

"It's in normal cases that they can decide who they want to live with," Christina joins the conversation. "But you understand that your mother is being pressured from all sides for political reasons."

It turns out that the girls decided to surprise me and planned this escape. After locking the door, happy, we sit in the kitchen and laugh. It seems that the worst of the ordeal is behind us.

But we are deeply mistaken. The Leviathan devours our lives at an incredible rate. In the evening it turned out that Arisha had been suddenly expelled from her home school, and her school papers had mysteriously disappeared.

The police refer to some strange order and force the child to go to another school, which is near her father's house on the other side of Moscow.

"I don't want to go to another school," my daughter cries. "I'm afraid that my dad will grab me again, take away my phone, and lock me up in his apartment."

Together with a lawyer, we try to return Arisha to her native school, where she has studied since the first grade, but each time we get refusals. Dmitry Zakhvatov sends endless complaints to the Department of Education and the prosecutor's office, but all in vain.

"I don't understand," I complain to the lawyer, "why would my ex-spouse abuse his own child? Any problems can be solved through negotiations, but he hides and doesn't want to talk. In a few years, when Putin's regime falls and the cult of personality is debunked, his daughter, now grown up, will come to him and ask, 'Daddy, why did you mock Mommy and me? Why did you forbid me to go abroad? Why didn't you want to talk to Mom? While she courageously opposed the war, you were her instigator....' And I think this will be the most frightening trial for him—communicating with his grown-up daughter."

"Everything that is happening to you is some kind of total lawlessness," Dmitry says, as indignant as I am. "I have never encountered anything like this in my legal practice. Can you imagine the security of your cottage village blocking the entrance to your house? I had to abandon my car and walk."

"How is it blocked? I pay for utilities; some of this money goes to their salaries." I am puzzled.

The problems are snowballing. Dmitry keeps writing complaints and appeals to various authorities, and Christina is trying to get Arisha back to her home school. But they, day after day, get rejection after rejection.

"What should I do?" Christina asks the lawyer. "I just got a call from an investigator and he called me in for questioning at the Investigative Committee too."

"Take a sick leave immediately; you just complained that you have a cold," Dmitry advises. "He probably decided to bring you in as an accomplice or a witness to the Marina crime. They probably looked at the CCTV footage and saw that you were filming with your phone the protest outside the Kremlin. Apparently, in this way they decided to put pressure on you and deprive Marina of all help."

Christina immediately rushes to the doctor to get a certificate of incapacity for work. And at the same time, the head of the territorial branch of the Federal Penitentiary Service comes to my house to check on me.

I open the door. On the threshold of the house stands a tall blond with a face disfigured by anger and hatred. The inspector has no more intimate conversations with me in her presence but acts exactly as instructed.

The two of them take me to the Moscow City Court building, where they will consider my lawyer's appeal against my illegal arrest. All the way there, I'm rereading George Orwell's *1984*. I don't keep my eyes on the road at all.

"Is that the Moscow City Court?" I look up in surprise.

"No, it's the Shcherbinsky Court," answers the warden.

It was like they poured a bucket of cold water on me. Not only are all the sessions on the article on fakes held behind closed doors, but in order to isolate me from journalists, they bring me to the outskirts of Moscow instead of the center of the city.

We enter the courthouse. Rosgvardia soldiers in bulletproof vests with the ominous letter *Z* are carefully checking my bag. Today they are working in a stepped-up mode. Putin has just announced the beginning of partial mobilization and the authorities are afraid of mass riots.

The judge of the Moscow City Court starts the session via video link. I'm sitting alone in an empty hall, holding a white sheet of paper with the words "No mobilization!" The words of the prosecutor come to me, once again stating that the dead children in Ukraine are fakes because their deaths are not reported by the Russian Ministry of Defense. My lawyer's arguments about my innocence are completely ignored.

The judge leaves the measure of restraint unchanged, in the form of house arrest. The journalists ask for a video feed of the trial, but it mysteriously disappears.

After the trial, my lawyer comes to my house.

"You have one last chance to save your life if you don't want to rot in jail," Dmitry explains. "You're losing precious time."

I understand his hint perfectly. I have to flee Russia. I'm having another nervous coughing fit.

It was the agony of a system that was losing on all fronts. Russian troops were rapidly retreating from Ukraine, hundreds of thousands of conscripted men were fleeing the country to escape mobilization, and the courts were stamping anti-war convictions in droves.

There is less and less time until October 10, when I have to stand before the Basmanny Court again. I have to save my life urgently. But I can't leave my daughter, and she doesn't have a passport. It's a vicious circle.

CHAPTER 23

ESCAPE

Salvation comes unexpectedly.

"Reporters Without Borders will help you in Europe," Christina tells me. "Your former colleague Zhanna Agalakova is in touch with them."

"Great," I yell, jumping to the ceiling with joy. I can hardly believe the reality of what's happening. It looks like my main problem has been solved.

"Now we're going to have an unusual geography lesson," I tell my daughter, excited by the good news, as I open the world map on my laptop. "What countries border Russia?"

"Estonia, Latvia, Lithuania," Arisha begins to list. "Belarus, Ukraine."

"And also Finland," I pick up, "Norway, Georgia, Azerbaijan, Kazakhstan, China, Mongolia, and even North Korea."

"Where will you run?" Christina joins in on our quiz.

"Probably North Korea," I said ironically.

We laugh.

"Yeah, also suggest Iran," Arisha continues through laughter, looking at the map of the Middle East. The idea of running away with a child seems really adventurous to me, but I don't see any other way out.

"We need a friend's help," I say. Christina calls my lawyer.

Trying to save us, in total secrecy, Dmitry Zakhvatov begins to develop a plan. We are sitting on pins and needles. Our fate is being decided, and we are in complete ignorance.

"Take only backpacks with you," Dmitry instructs us.

We have a nervous tantrum. On the floor there are three suitcases that are almost full. One is gigantic; the rest are smaller. Documents, summer things, winter things, shoes....

"We can't go only with backpacks," I whine.

The lawyer nods understandingly. He picks up one huge suitcase and carries it to his car, promising that he will send our things on the first plane.

"By the way," Dmitry says, "Don't just sit and wait but start training. You need good physical form to cross the border illegally."

Arisha goes for a run, and I have no choice but to pedal on my home exercise bike because I'm still under house arrest. My mind paints the bleakest pictures of illegal migrants from Africa and the Middle East trying to get into the European Union by boats.

Finally, the decisive day arrives. Friday night is the best time to escape. The workweek is over. The guards of order are at the dacha with vodka and shish kebabs. For the first time I am glad that all law enforcement and security agencies in Russia are a real mess. By the weekend no one will be looking for me. When the investigator gets to work on Monday, he will be informed that I escaped, and only then will he put me on the federal wanted list. We have at least a two-day lead.

I sit down on the couch and record a video message.

"Dear officers of the Federal Penitentiary Service. Put this bracelet on Putin; it is him, not me, who should be isolated from society and tried for the genocide of the people of Ukraine and for the fact that he is mass murdering the male population of Russia."

If all goes well, I will publish this appeal on my social networks when I am outside of Russia.

It's 10:30 p.m., and we are already standing with our suitcases outside, but at that moment the gate opens, and my mother enters the yard. She watches me more closely than the officers of the FSIN.

"What's that strange car standing outside the house at this late hour?" she asks, clearly suspecting something is wrong.

As I go, I make up a story that people came to me with the papers from the lawyer. At this point the girls quickly hide their suitcases in the bathroom. Christina sends a message to the driver to pull away from the house and wait for us around the corner.

"You're a criminal now." My mother stares at my leg with an electronic bracelet. "Whatever you do, Putin will destroy all the Nazis in Ukraine anyway."

"Mom, do you realize that if the rhetoric in the state media changes now and they start telling you that Ukrainians and Americans are the best people on earth, your opinion will change dramatically?" Once again I try to talk sense into my mother.

But she doesn't listen. She slams the door loudly in farewell and leaves.

After making sure no one's around, Christina and Arisha jump out into the street and run to the waiting car. Pulling a black cap over my eyes, I rush after them. We throw our things in the trunk and drive off. The signals from my electronic bracelet no longer reach the base stations. To cover our tracks, we change the car at the nearest vacant lot.

"Oh, I forgot to cut the bracelet off," I suddenly remember.

I know the bracelet doesn't have a tracking device, but it's better to get rid of it right now. I rummage around in the bottom of my purse, among the cream tubes, perfume bottles, and lipstick, and find the pre-prepared wire cutters. I try to cut the strap off, but I don't succeed the first time. There are metal threads inside the strap.

"Damn it," I shout in despair.

I squeeze the wire cutters even harder, and the metal strands tear. I take off the bracelet and throw it with all my might onto the roadside.

"Long live freedom!" I shout in triumph.

"Hooray!" the girls say.

The driver clearly does not understand what is going on but does not ask unnecessary questions. I ask him to stop for a couple of minutes on the outskirts. Christina is leaving us for a while. As soon as possible, she promises to fly us to Europe with our suitcases. On the wide highway, the car takes us farther and farther away from Moscow.

After a few hours, a thick fog descends on the road, and the driver slows down. My daughter puts her head in my lap, and we fall into an anxious sleep.

In the afternoon, we stop in a remote village. The squalid houses peek out through the yellowing foliage.

"My part of the journey is over," the driver says tiredly. "I have brought you to the designated point. Another car should be waiting for you here."

At that moment, an old gray Lada comes around the corner. Leaving puffs of gray dust on the road, it pulls up beside us. Without asking too many questions, we jump in and drive on.

Five minutes later, the driver pulls into the open gate. In the yard of the house there is a huge Caucasian shepherd dog on a chain, which starts barking loudly at our appearance.

"Shut up; these are our own people," the owner yells at him.

The dog becomes silent and starts wagging his tail good-naturedly.

"Call me Anton," our companion introduces himself in a whisper as we enter the house. "I'll be your guide across the border. We'll wait until it gets dark, and then we'll try to cross the border. We may not succeed at the first attempt. But don't be afraid. I'm a local here and I know all the roads."

I nod understandingly, not yet fully aware of what lies ahead. A few hours later, a small Renault pulls into the courtyard. Our guide sits next to the driver. We are placed in the back. The car loops along a small gravel road between fields and farms.

In the distance we notice the burning headlights of a car standing on the side of the road.

"Let's move quickly," Anton says curtly, and his tension is transmitted to us. "Now comes the border, the hardest part of the journey."

He throws our stuff into the trunk of a rusty car. Bouncing on the bumps, the car rushes straight through a field of dry grass. An elderly man in absorbent cotton is behind the wheel. Suddenly the trunk of the car opens, and out of the corner of my eye I see my black backpack fall out onto the road.

"Pull over," I yell to the driver.

Anton jumps out of the car, picks up the backpack, and slams the trunk shut. But the driver can't move; the car is stuck in the mud. Suddenly two lights appear. They seem to be the headlights of a car coming our way.

"There's not much left." The driver quickly puts out the headlights. "Run over there." He waves his hand somewhere in the distance. It's pitch black all around.

We grab our backpacks and suitcases from the trunk and run.

"We were told that we would have to walk seven hundred meters," I try to ask Anton.

"Maybe a little more."

Suddenly I step into a deep hole. I can't see anything, but I realize that the ground in front of us is plowed. Apparently, a tractor had recently passed through here and left behind huge boulders. After taking a few steps, we stop.

"I can't go any farther," whines Arisha.

The headlights of a moving car are approaching.

"Get down, heads down," Anton commands. "It's the border guards."

All three of us fall to the ground. Afraid to move, we lay there watching the approaching spotlights. Suddenly they stop and then start moving in the opposite direction.

"It's a tractor," I guess.

We jump up from the damp ground and, stumbling, run on.

"Come on, come on; girls, hurry up," Anton urges us.

After three hundred meters, we stop to catch our breath.

"Mom, give me some water," Arisha asks, shaking lumps of earth out of her sneakers.

I give her the last two sips of water that were left at the bottom of the plastic bottle.

Another four hours pass. All this time we are looping through a plowed field, constantly hiding from the tractors. Ahead of us is a dense forest, with the lights of a settlement on the horizon to the left.

"Anton, according to my calculations, we've already walked five kilometers in the field, not seven hundred meters," I say incredulously. "Where have you led us?"

"Girls, pull yourself together," Anton whispers, breathing heavily. "It's hard for me, too. I'm carrying your two suitcases. They're waiting for us there."

He points toward the woods.

But we are finally exhausted and do not respond to his calls. We seem to have reached the limit of our human capabilities. And we can't even move.

"Take me back to Moscow," Arisha whines. "My feet hurt."

"And I'd rather go to jail than take another step," I exclaim in anger.

My mind paints the bleakest pictures. I think about the fact that if one of us breaks a leg in the darkness now, we won't get out of here until dawn. And in the morning the border guards will catch us. After my prosperous life in Moscow, everything that happens to me reminds me of some kind of endless horror movie. It seems like I'm about to wake up and it will all disappear.

Anton takes out his phone and tries to get a signal. There is no connection.

"Let's go; we have to get out of the lowland," he says.

We get up and follow him across the field, constantly falling into holes. After five hundred meters, Anton whispers happily, "We have a signal!"

He drops his suitcases and dials a number.

"Where are you? Turn on the lights; we can't see you," he says into the phone.

It's still pitch black in the woods.

"We're going to the brightest star, the yellow one, and behind us is the tail of the Big Dipper." Anton raises his head to the sky. "To our right are the lights of two tractors, and to our left, it looks like another tractor or car."

"They're on their way to us," Anton whispers.

Near the forest, we notice the light of a hand flashlight. We rush toward it with cheer.

But at least another half hour passes before we meet a man all in black. He picks up our things and strides confidently toward the woods.

It's getting easier to walk. The plowing is finally over. We enter the forest, and our feet get stuck in the swamp.

"Girls, we have to walk through the woods a little more, and there will be the border," says the stranger. "Try to walk on the bumps. I'll walk ahead and shine my flashlight."

We walk, gritting our teeth.

After an hour, the road is blocked by barbed wire poles.

"This way," the stranger says quietly, lifting up the wire.

Arisha squats and climbs into the hole first. I crawl after. Several prickly thorns pierce my palms at once, but I feel no pain because I am already so tired.

After a good half kilometer, we see an old car standing on a forest road. We fall down on the back seat and greedily drink water.

"I feel like I've just swam the Bosporus twice, or finished a half Ironman. It was the best training I've ever had," I joke bitterly.

"Yes, a race in the mud with obstacles and suitcases," Arisha comments on our adventure, looking at her black palms.

We laugh, but our laughter is more like hysteria. The car pulls into the courtyard of a house on the outskirts of the village. An elderly woman comes out to meet us. After a quick glance at us, she leads us into the bathroom. We spend more than an hour trying to get our suitcases and shoes clean.

"It's dangerous to stay here; the border is too close. Everyone knows each other in this village," Anton explains. "Now we'll eat and go on our way."

It's starting to get light outside. We sit in the back of a black Ford and instantly fall asleep.

"Here we are; this is the end point of our journey." Anton wakes us up. "I was told to bring you here."

"How so?" I ask. "We have to go to the capital."

Anton shrugs his shoulders. He leads us into a one-story brick house and tells us to wait. Inside we are not alone. Russian speech can be heard from the next room.

It turns out that three guys from Moscow live there. They fled to escape the mobilization. Anton asks me not to leave the room because they might recognize me. The Internet is already full of messages about my escape.

Without thinking twice, I find a driver online who agrees to go right now.

"I'm already confused as to which car it is," Arisha says in surprise as she gets into the silver SUV.

"This is the seventh, and hopefully the last," I clarify.

On the third day after our escape, we drive up to a huge residence. Hiding our faces from the video cameras, we quickly run inside. They are already waiting for us there. For the first time we feel safe and secure.

EPILOGUE

A Russian court restricted my parental rights. The court ruling stated that the children should live with their father because "the mother is engaged in political activity." I have no doubt that the verdict was dictated from above.

Fortunately, at that time I was already outside of Russia, which PACE and the European Parliament had recognized as a state sponsor of terrorism. I was standing in the middle of a small airport with my suitcase. We were moving from one country to another. I can't reveal all the details of my escape yet. But I hope that someday, when Russia shakes off the morass of Putinism and becomes part of the free world again, there will be something to tell. I assure you, life is more interesting than the most exciting political detective.

A black car loops through the narrow, busy streets of Paris. We drive to the office of Reporters Without Borders. Their options in the story of our rescue were indeed limitless.

"Put your mask on," a man's voice interrupted my musings. "We'll go through the archway, and another car will be waiting for us there."

As I get into the other car, I sink back into my thoughts.

The war turned my life upside down for the second time. First Russian troops wiped out my home in Grozny. Now the

Kremlin has deprived me not only of my home, but also of my family and my homeland. But it couldn't take away the most important thing—my freedom.

I don't know how soon this war will end and what lies ahead for me. I am not sure that I will be able to hug my mother and son anytime soon or that I will even be able to return to my home, which I built with so much labor and love. But I am firmly convinced that no one will ever make me lie again and justify the numerous crimes of the Putin regime.

"Mom," my daughter's cheerful voice interrupts my heavy thoughts. "Remember the last time we were in France, I threw coins into all the fountains of Paris. Then I made a wish to come here again..."

"I hope you wished for a flight from Moscow to Paris, not an overnight escape through fields, forests, and marshes."

Arisha laughs out loud. I look at her and think about how my daughter is my motivation to keep going and not give up. Sometimes I blame myself for putting her through such a huge ordeal. Perhaps for the sake of preserving the comfort of our family life it would have been easier for me to hide my head in the sand, like millions of Russians do, and pretend that nothing awful is going on.

But silence is complicity in a crime. When Russian bombs began to fall on Ukrainian cities, it was impossible to sit quietly and be silent. Someone had to stand up and tell the world, just as in Hans Christian Anderson's fairy tale, loudly: "The king is naked!" Putin has built this propaganda factory around himself, a factory of absolute lies, but it's just cardboard scenery to cover his nakedness and helplessness. And these decorations will soon collapse, and the moment of epiphany that will eventually come for Russians will be deafeningly awful. They will realize that Putin has in fact committed treason and destroyed Russia, depriving them of a normal future. His policies have been based on constant lies, manipulation, and overpowering hypocrisy!

All of his stated goals for the war have failed, and Russia has become a rogue state with a declining economy and a deteriorating demographic situation. Russia is now the world's terrorist state, from which a constant military threat emanates, and for the sake of counteracting which we must unite. Just as the word "Germany" was once associated not with Goethe, Bach, or the great German scientists, but with the mad Hitler, the Nazis, and the Holocaust. And so today, behind everything to which the adjective "Russian" can be applied, there is only death, destruction, aggression, and lies. And that's for the long haul!

The comparisons between Putin and Hitler, and modern Russia and the Third Reich, are all too obvious. Most of all, Russia now resembles Germany in 1944; the military defeat of the Führer was still to come, but Germany and German culture as the world has known them for centuries no longer existed. Strange as it may seem, Germany was reborn. Maybe Russia can, too. At least, I very much hope so!

Our car stops outside a small building in the center of Paris. We go up the steep stairs with Christophe Deloire to the second floor. In the office of Reporters Sans Frontières is a wall of journalists. Dozens of video cameras are pointed at us:

Christophe starts talking first:

> "This operation took place in the strictest secrecy. I only called the journalist by the codename 'Evelina.' And I want to say thank you to everyone who helped us in this operation. Unfortunately, I can't tell you all the names. The escape of Marina and her daughter is a success. It's comparable to escaping over the Berlin

> Wall. And I apologize to those who called us and wanted to know information about Marina, but I could not disclose it at that time. Marina arrived on French soil in October. We cannot say exactly where or how she entered France. We helped her with everything. When she first arrived, we found her a house in the countryside. Then she changed several hotels. We gave her medical care, organized transfers.
>
> On March 15, the day after Marina went live, President Emmanuel Macron publicly announced that he was offering her political asylum. This communication was contained and we thank the French authorities for that. It is an honor for France to welcome here people like Marina Ovsyannikova, who embodies resistance to Russian propaganda.
>
> I would like to remind you that after Putin came to power:
>
> 37 Russian journalists were killed,
> Nineteen journalists are now in prison,
> 200 media outlets are recognized as foreign agents, 7 have been declared undesirable organizations, 10,000 sites are blocked."

The vivid speech of the head of RSF gives me confidence. Taking the microphone in my hands, I begin my speech:

> "We are meeting today on a tragic day! Right from the morning Russian troops have been shelling the entire territory of Ukraine. And first, of course, I want to express my overwhelming

> support for the heroic people of Ukraine. It's been almost a year now that they are fighting for their land, they are fighting for our future, they are fighting for the future of the entire civilized world. I wish the Ukrainians victory and the return of all their territories, only then will we be able to say that the criminal Putin regime will collapse and Russia can get rid of Putinism and return to civilized society."

Within an hour I am answering all the journalists' questions in detail. I thank the French authorities, Reporters without Borders, and the many, many people who helped us in this difficult time. I am eternally grateful to them. Thinking of them makes me smile. They are my confidence that evil cannot win, that power is on the side of light.

Printed in Great Britain
by Amazon

46785440R00106